I celebrate 25 years of professional tattooing in January of 2018. Tattooing has given me everything and I'm greatful to be apart of it. I've compiled these illustrations from 2017 in a volume A-E with 4 more volumes to follow. Hope you enjoy.

-Jason Freeman

I0500442

Note* *Please only use this book as a reference to inspire ideas and **do not copy** and tattoo these images.*

Wolf Wizard Press©
150 Ridge Street
Reno, NV 89509

Edited by: Jason Freeman

Made in the USA.

jfreemantattoo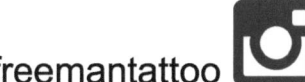

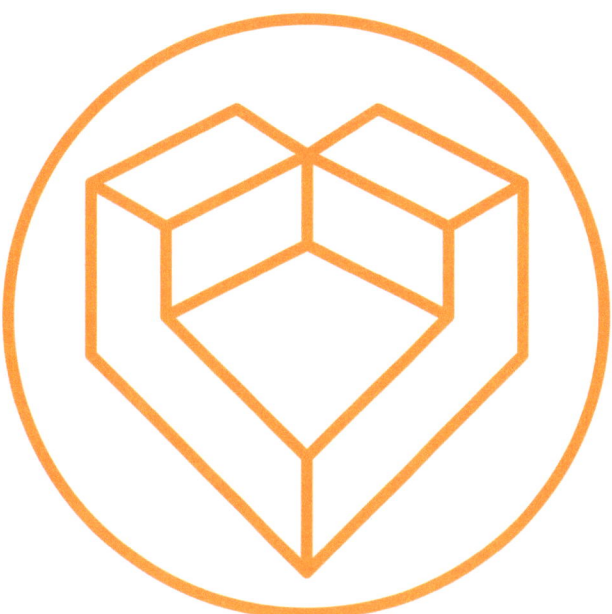

Dedicated to my son Kane.

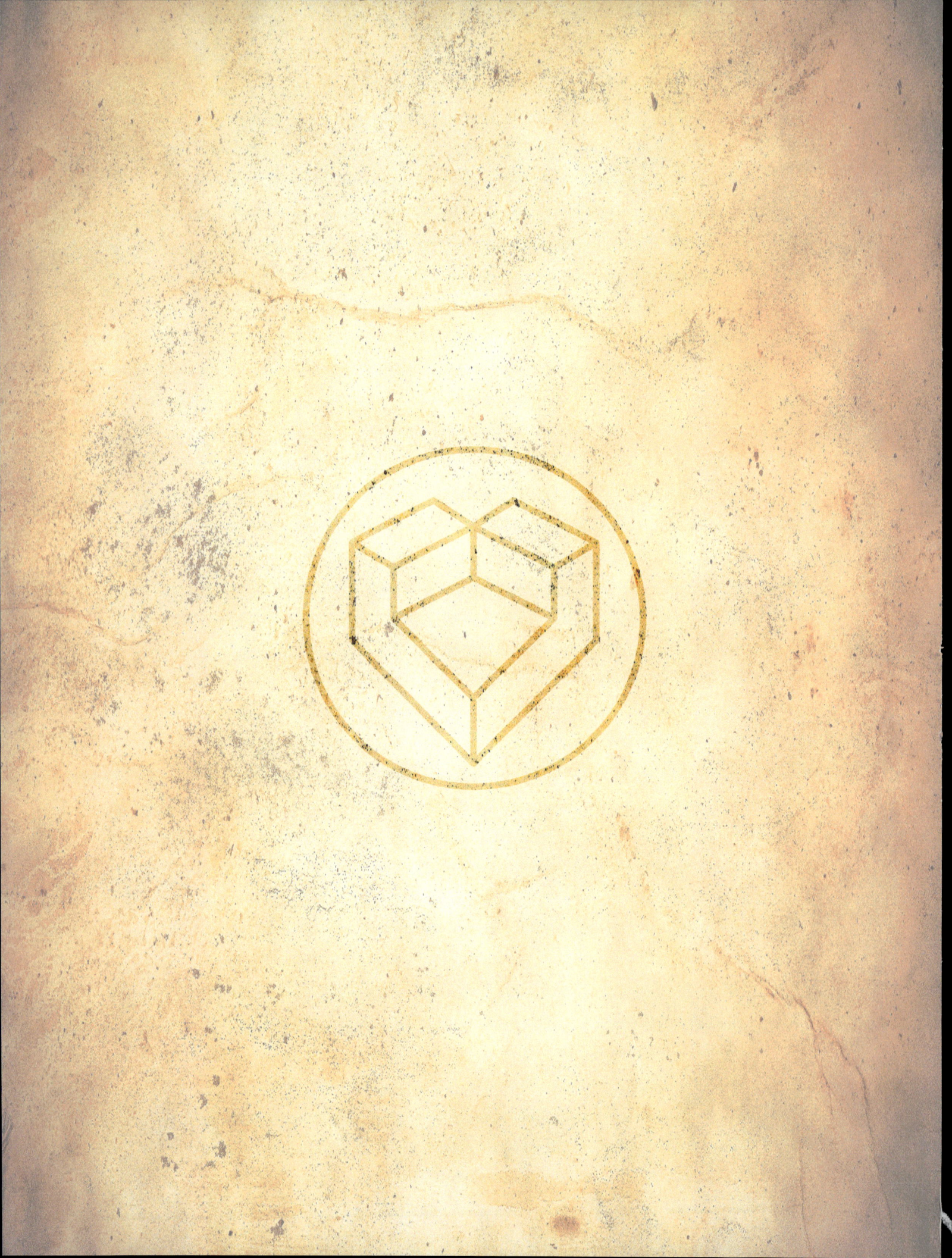

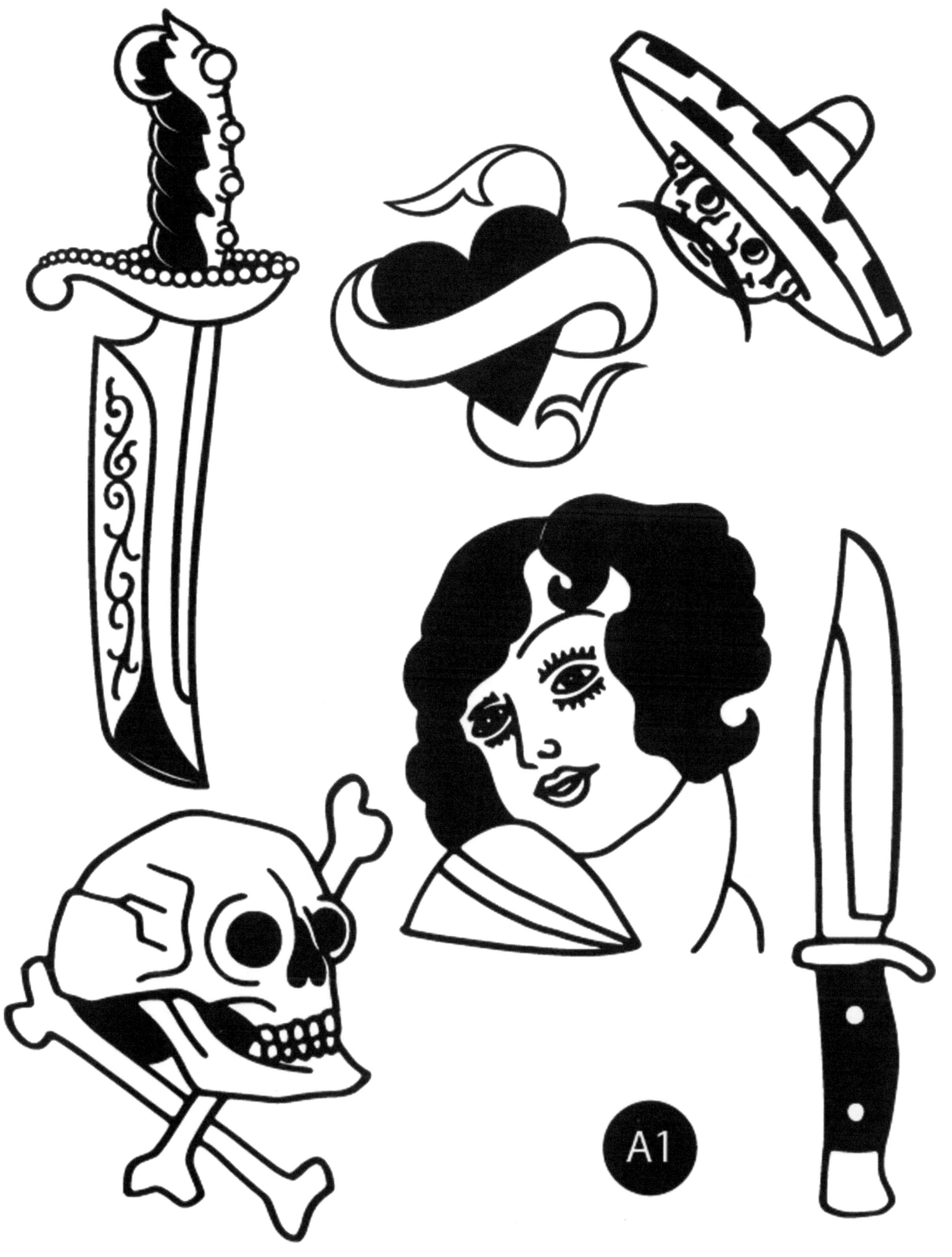

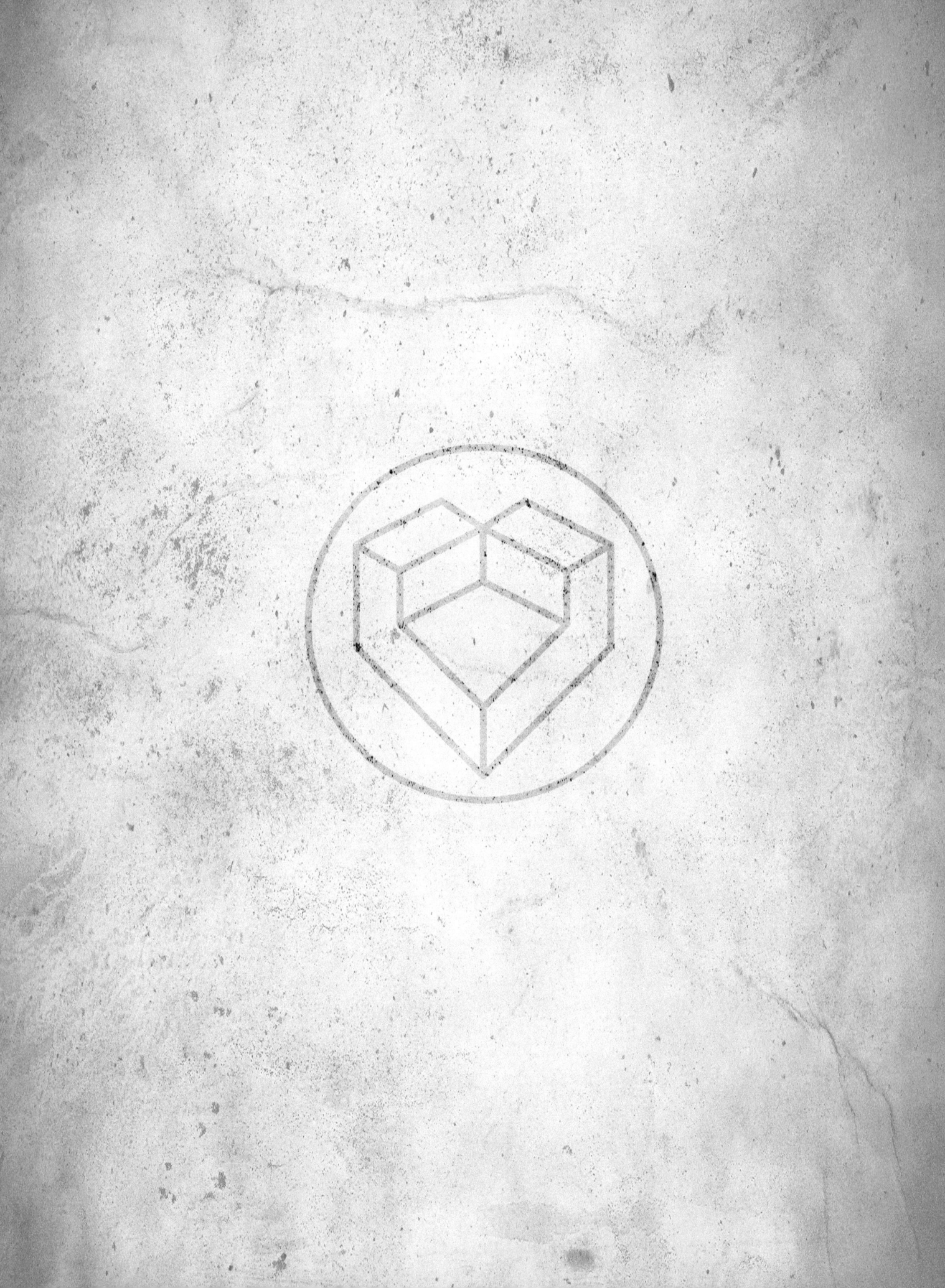

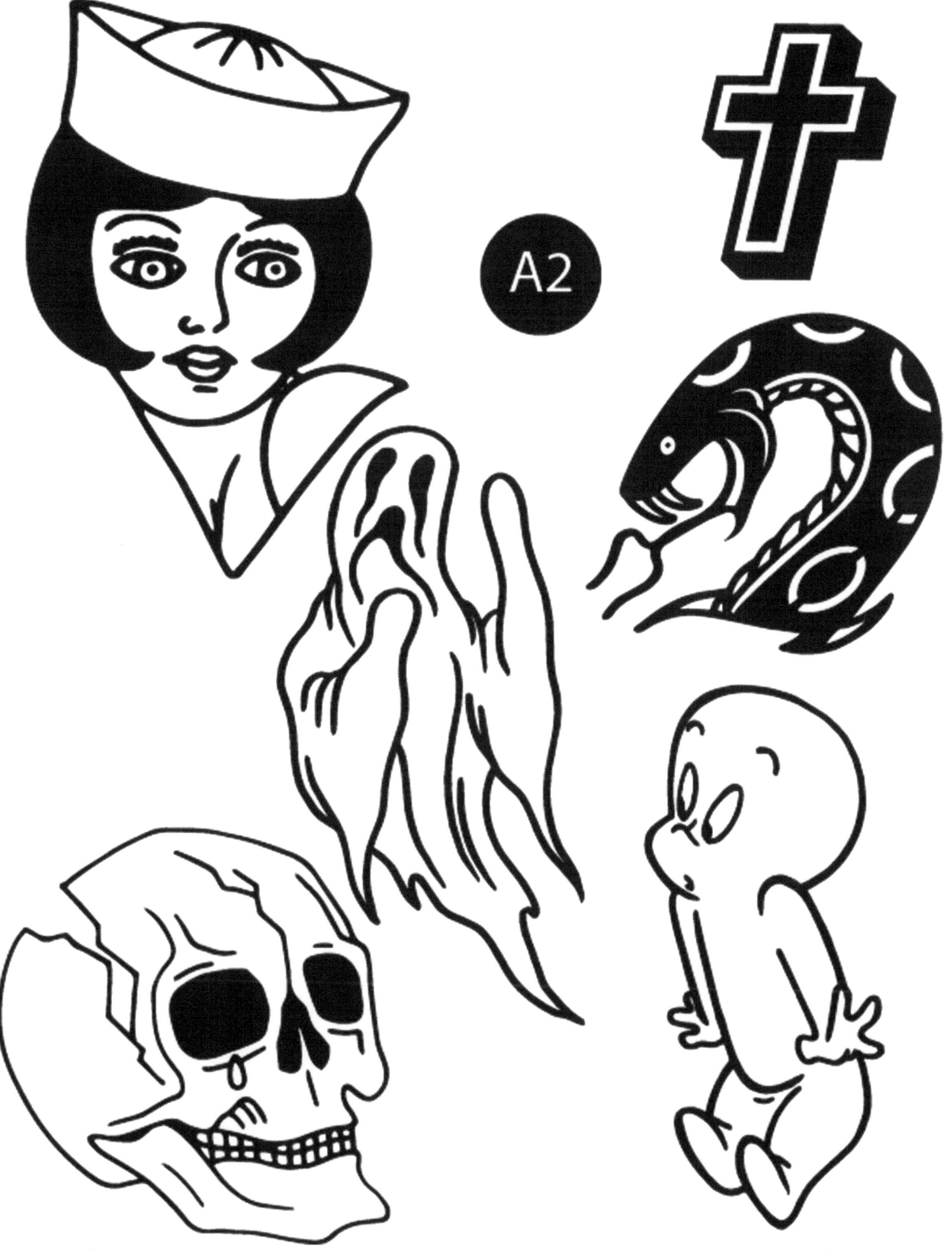

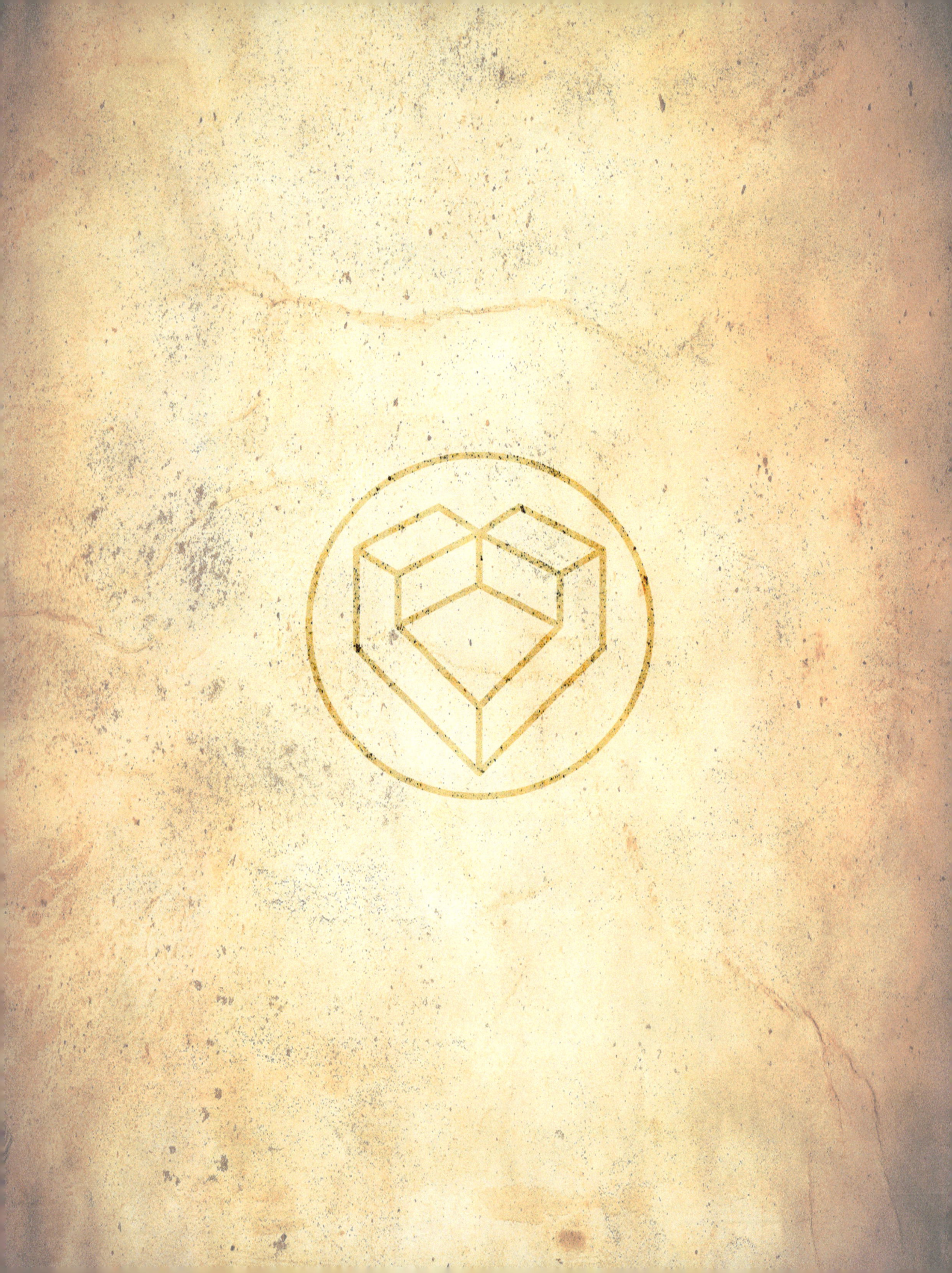

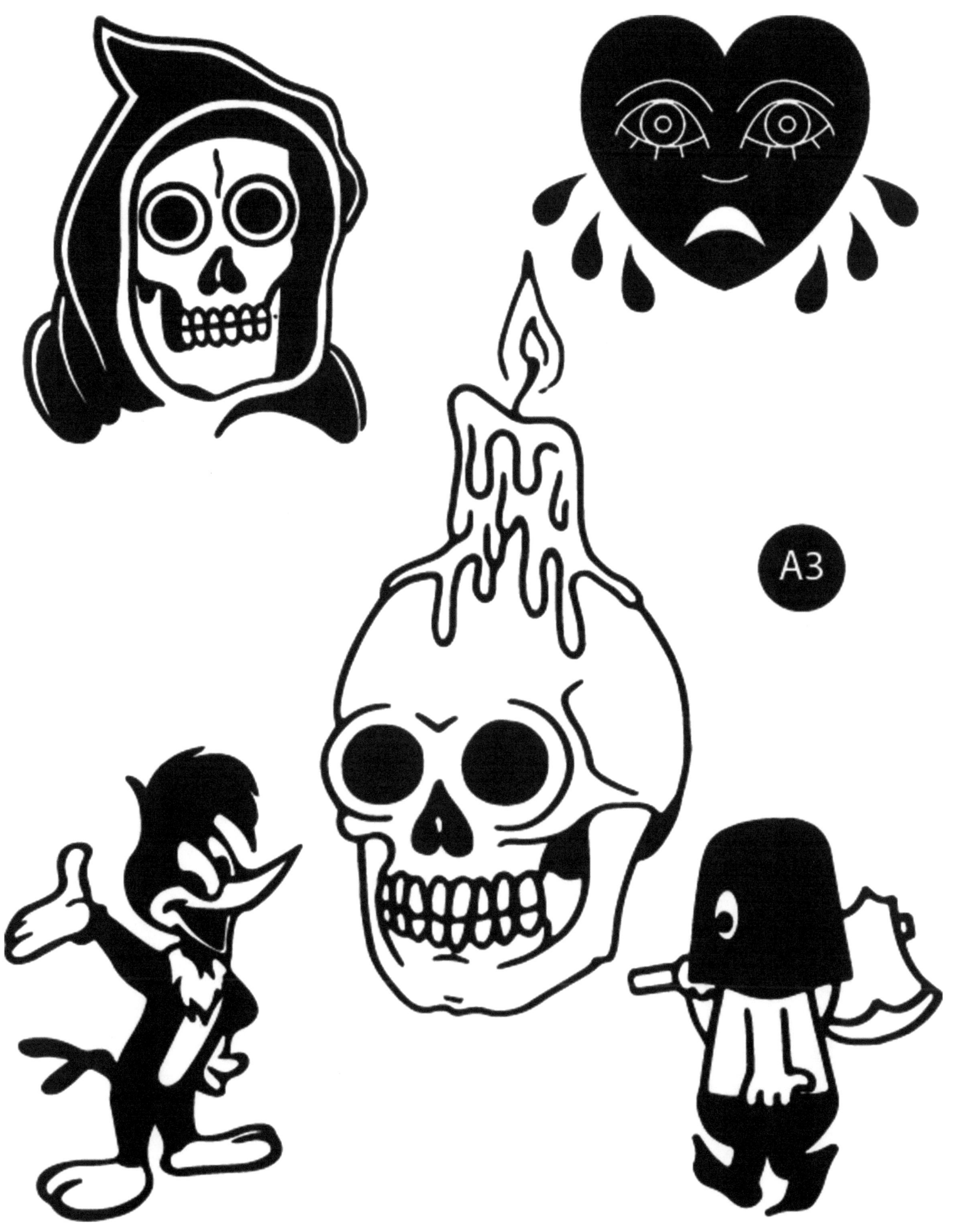

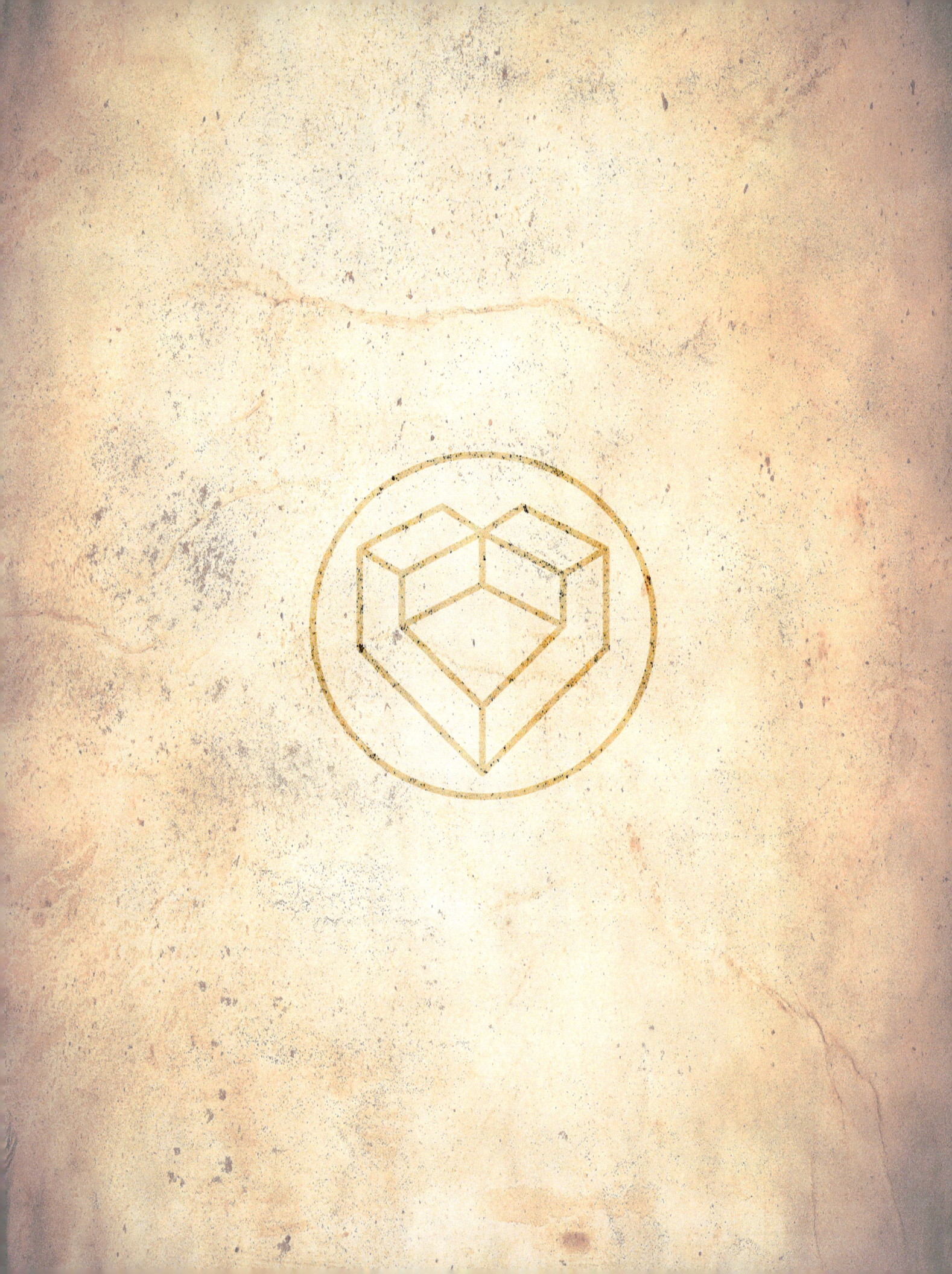

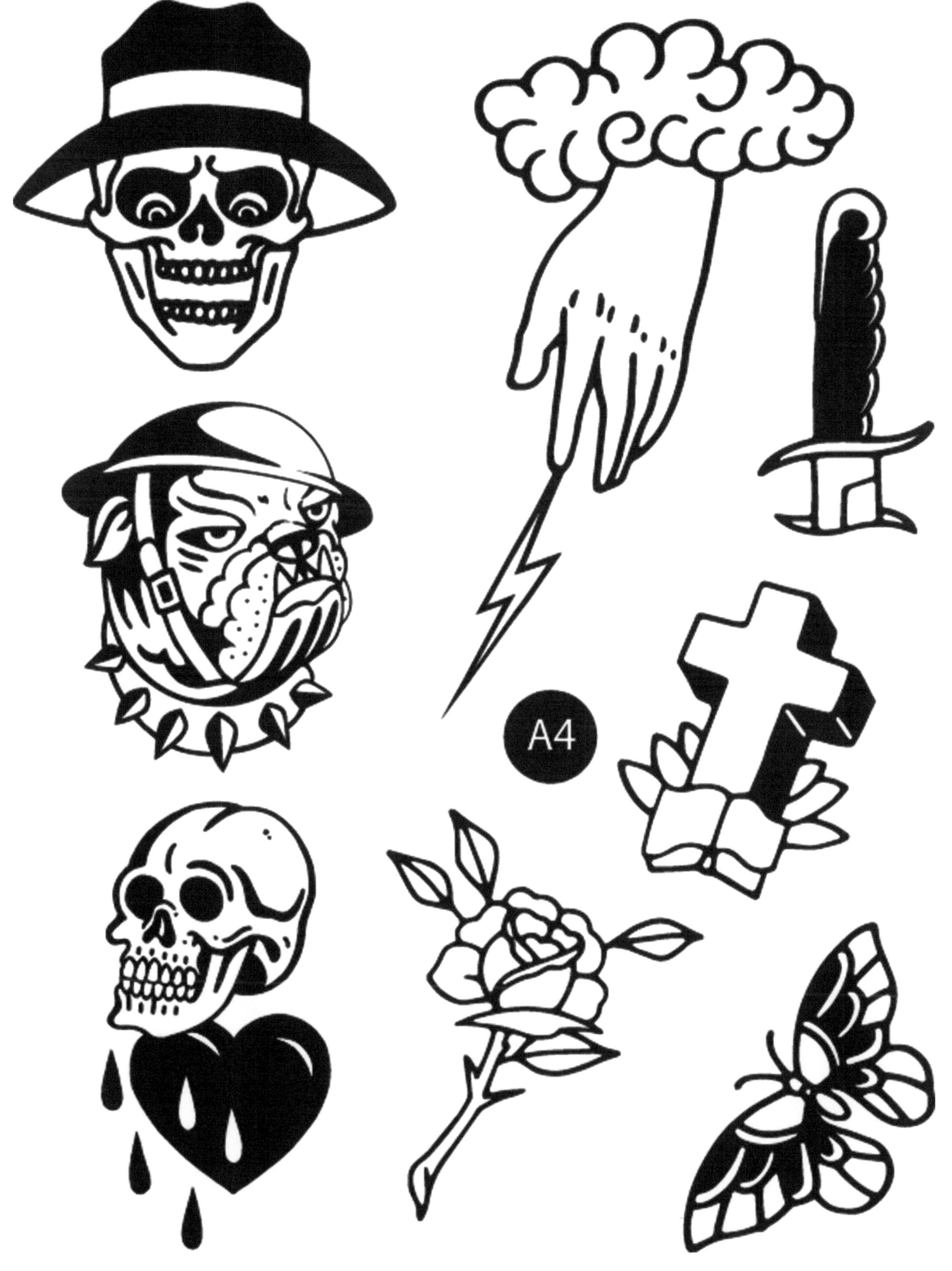

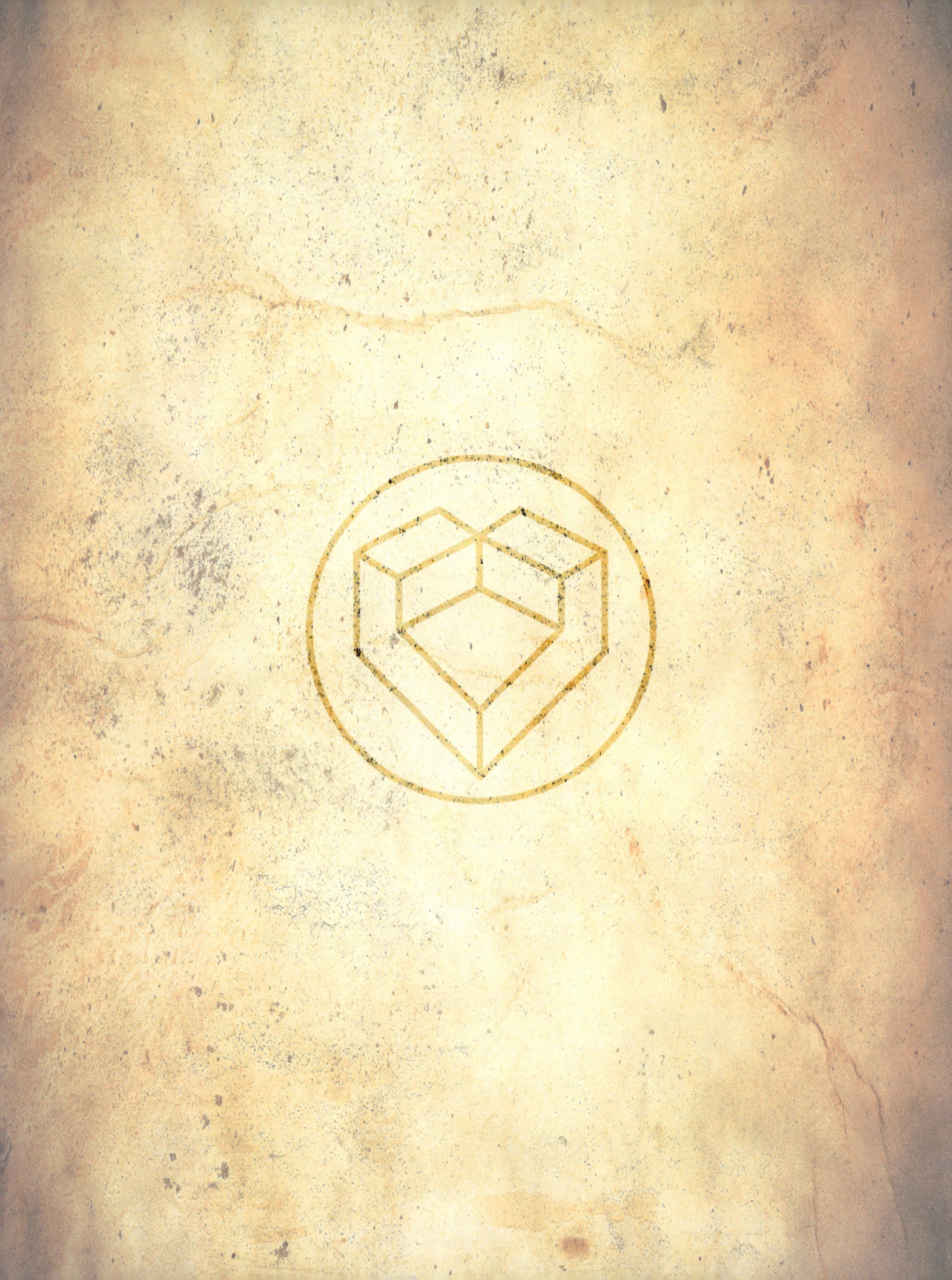

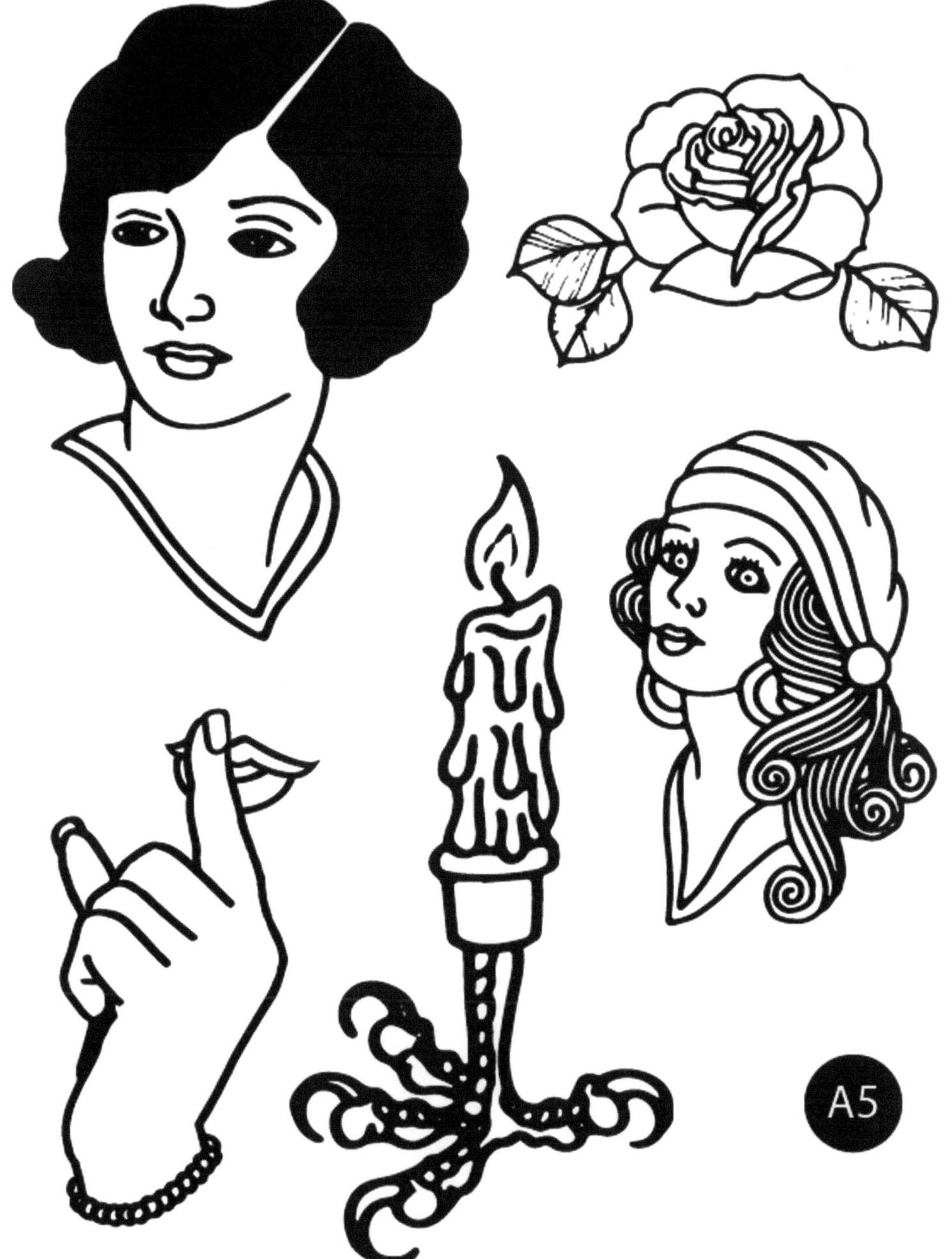

A5

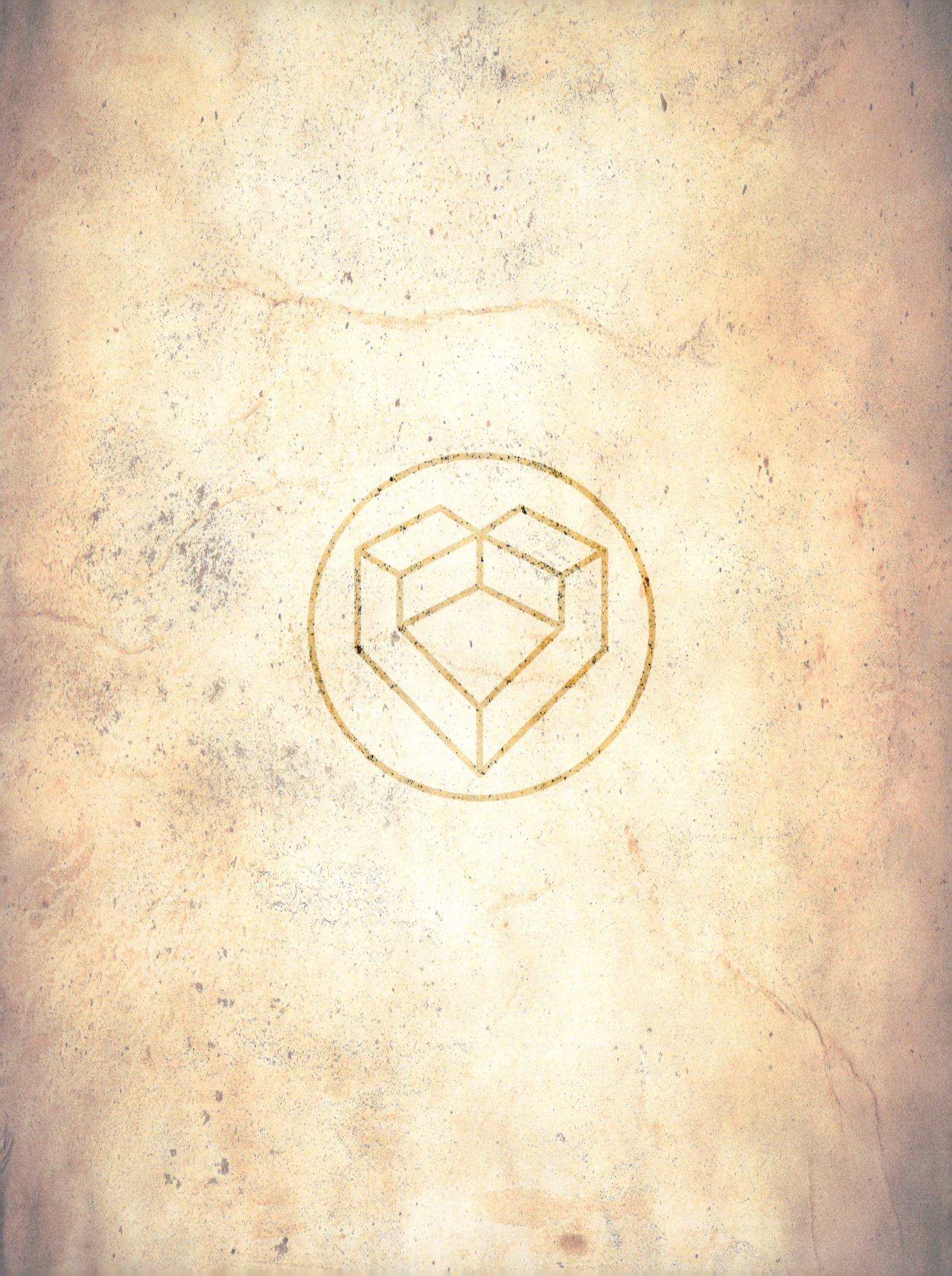

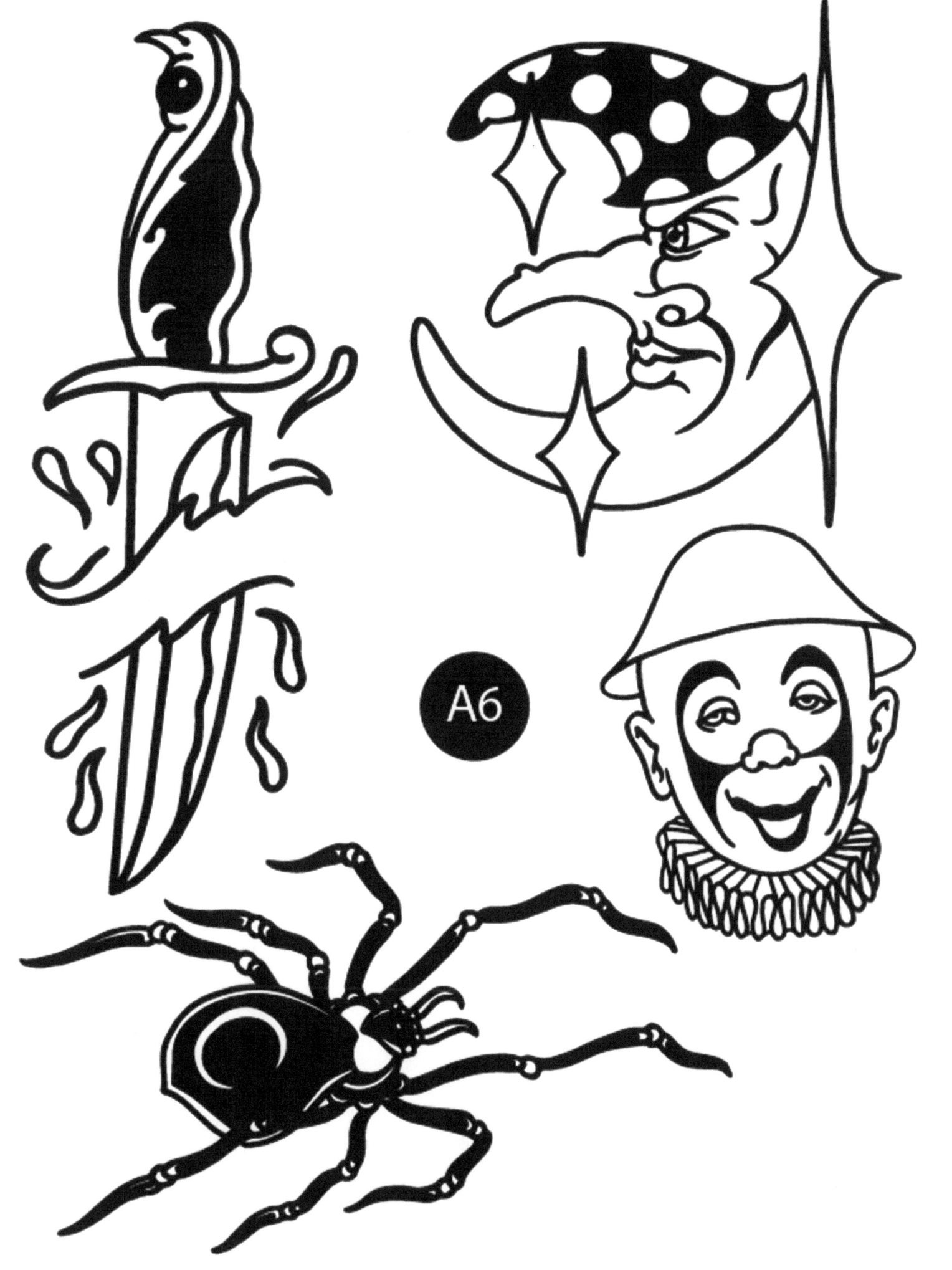

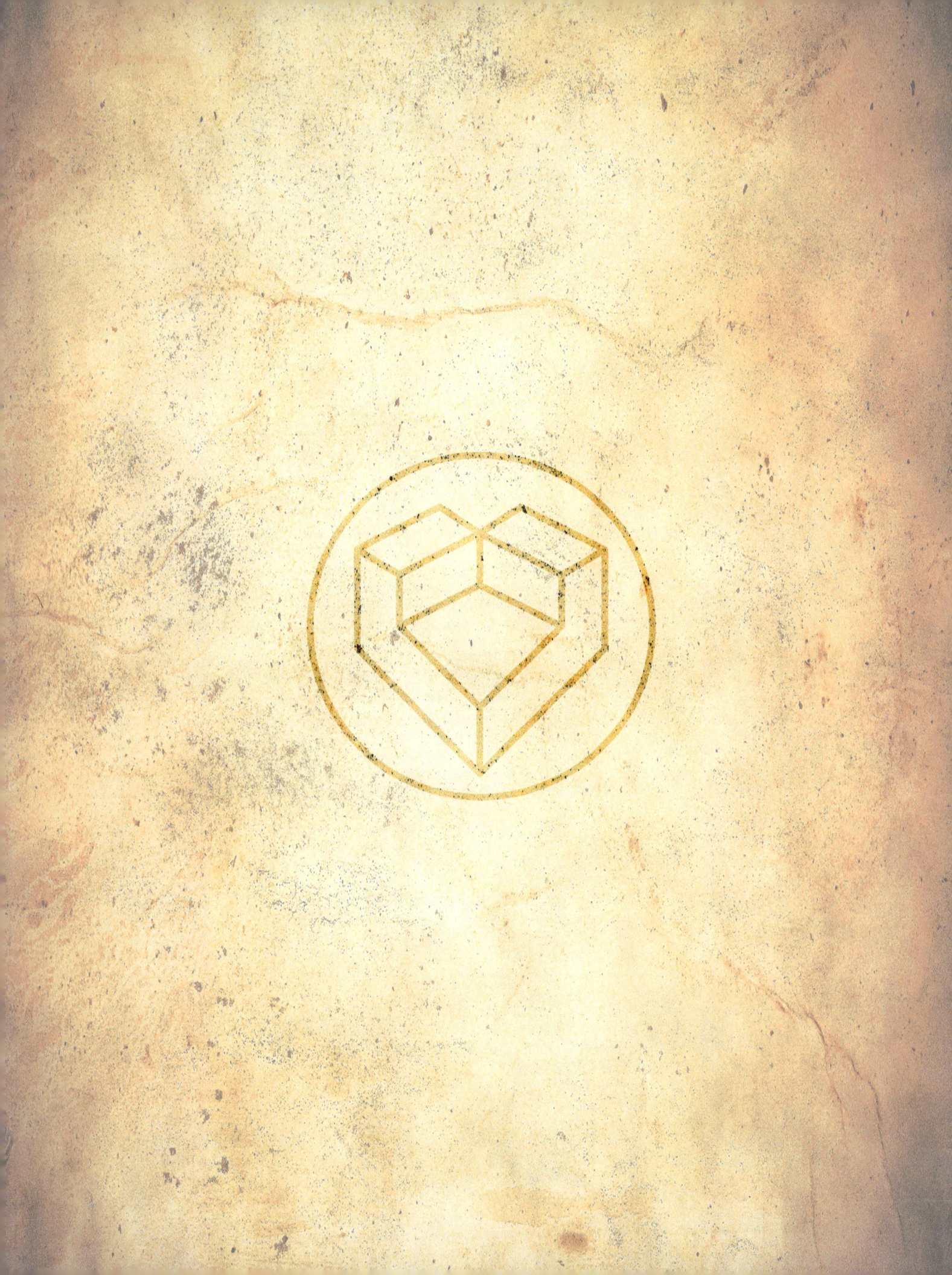

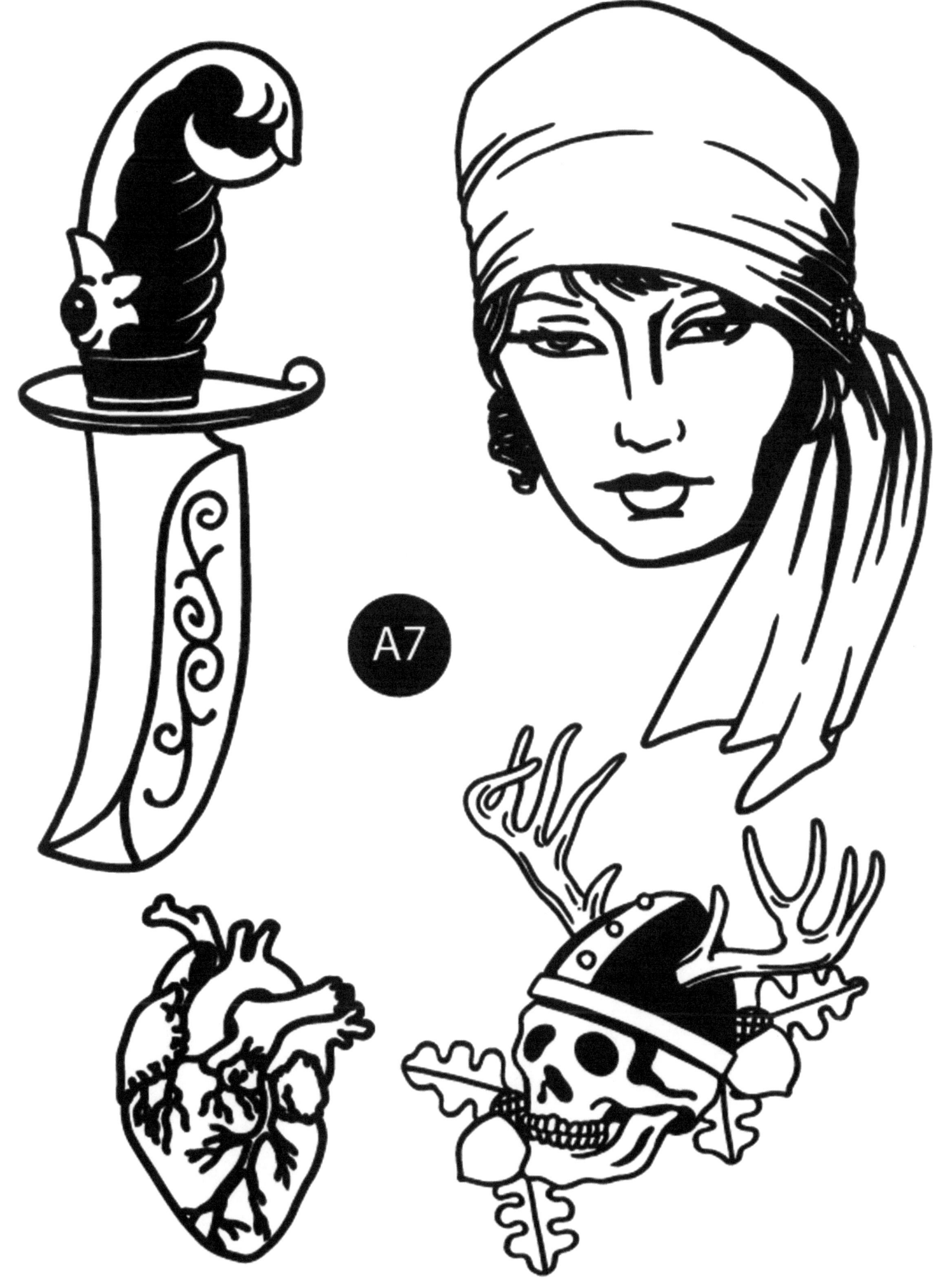

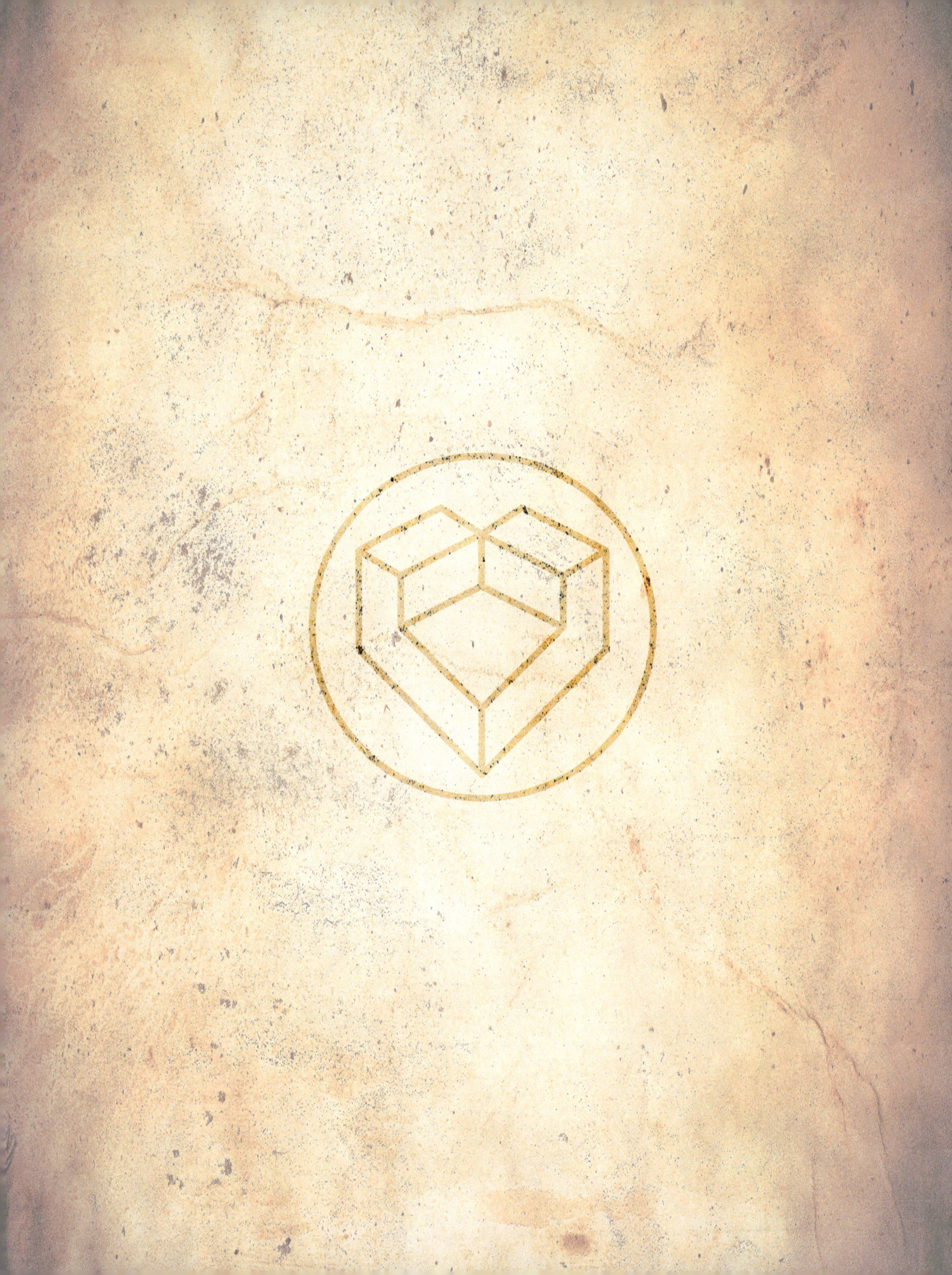

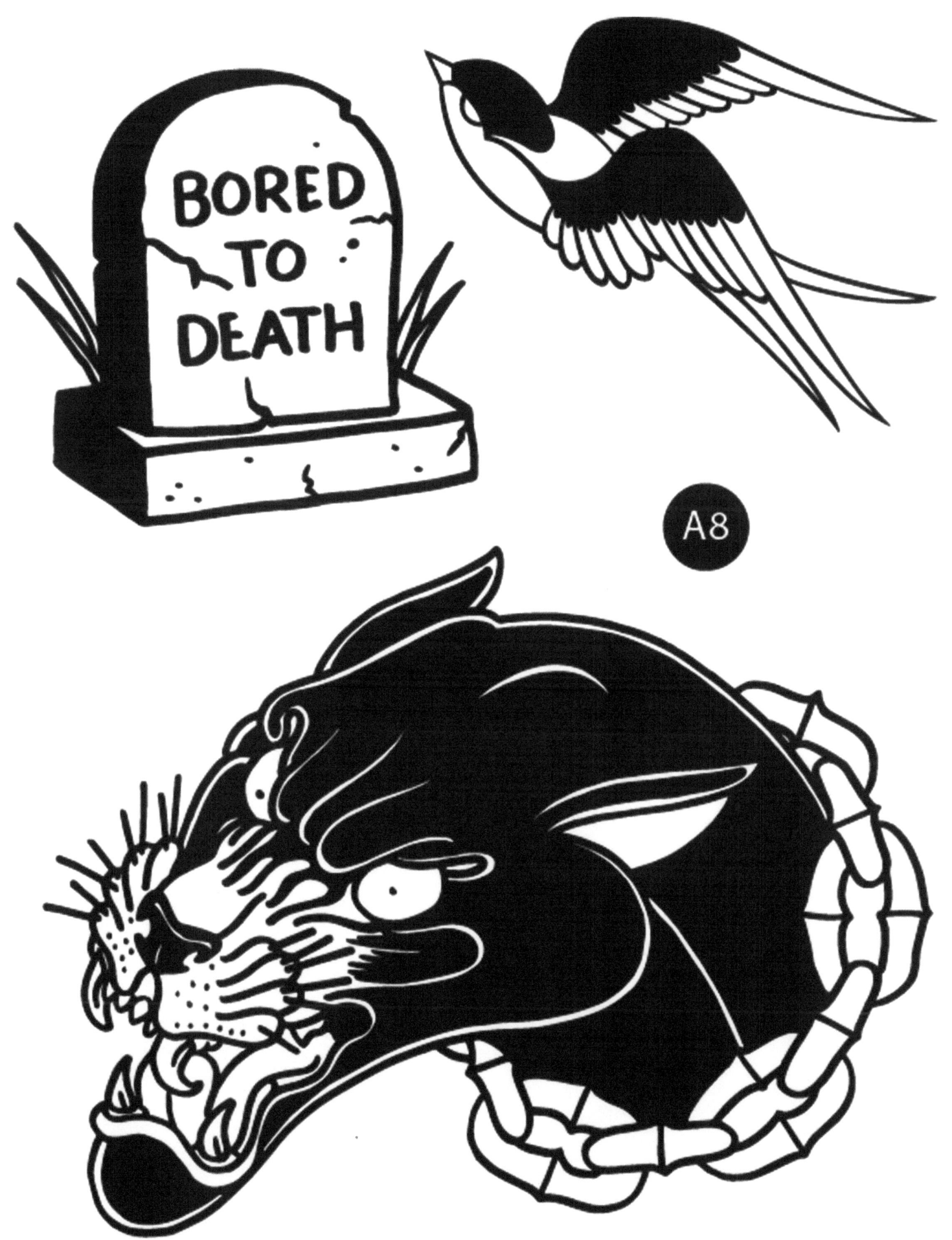

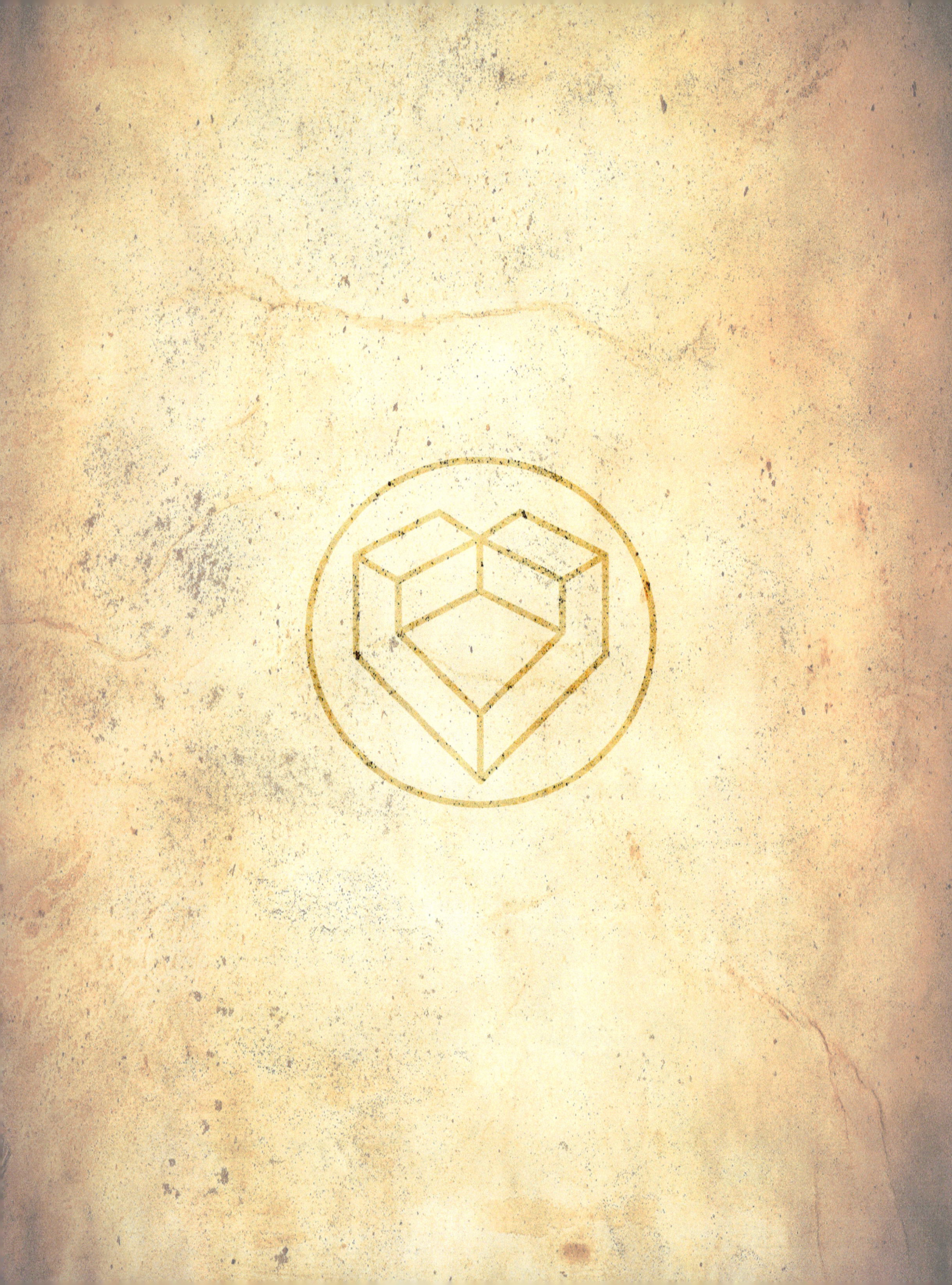

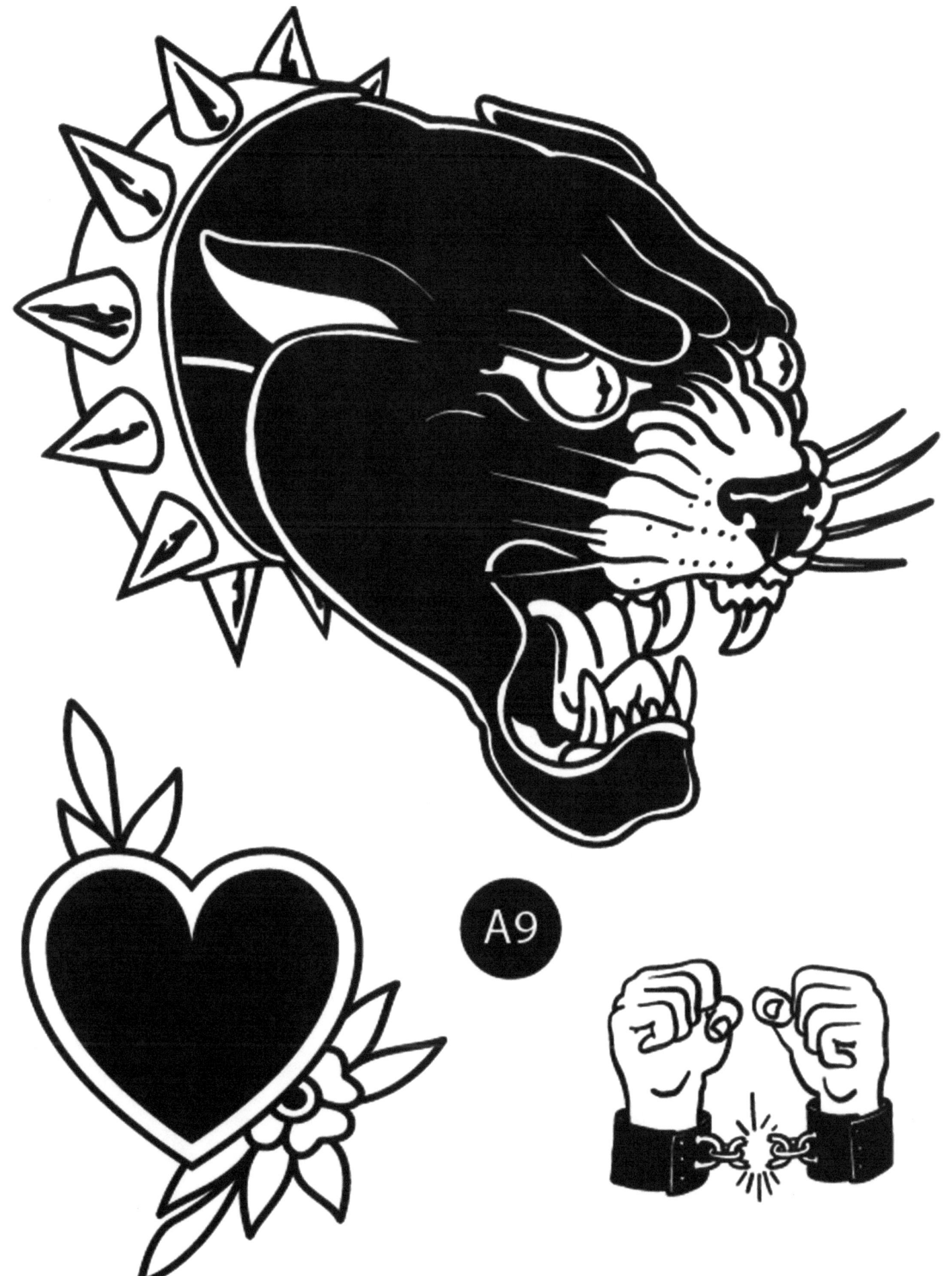

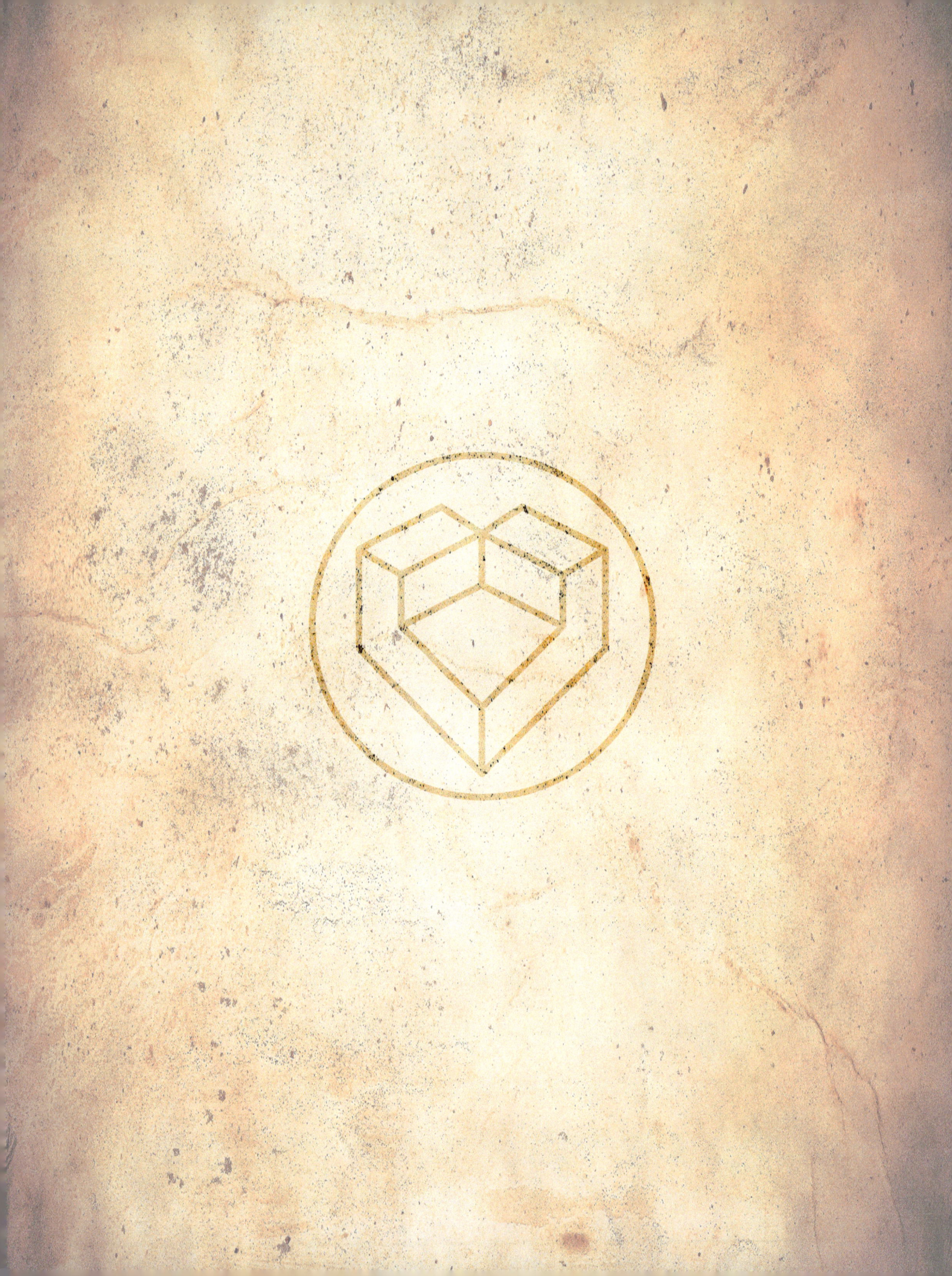

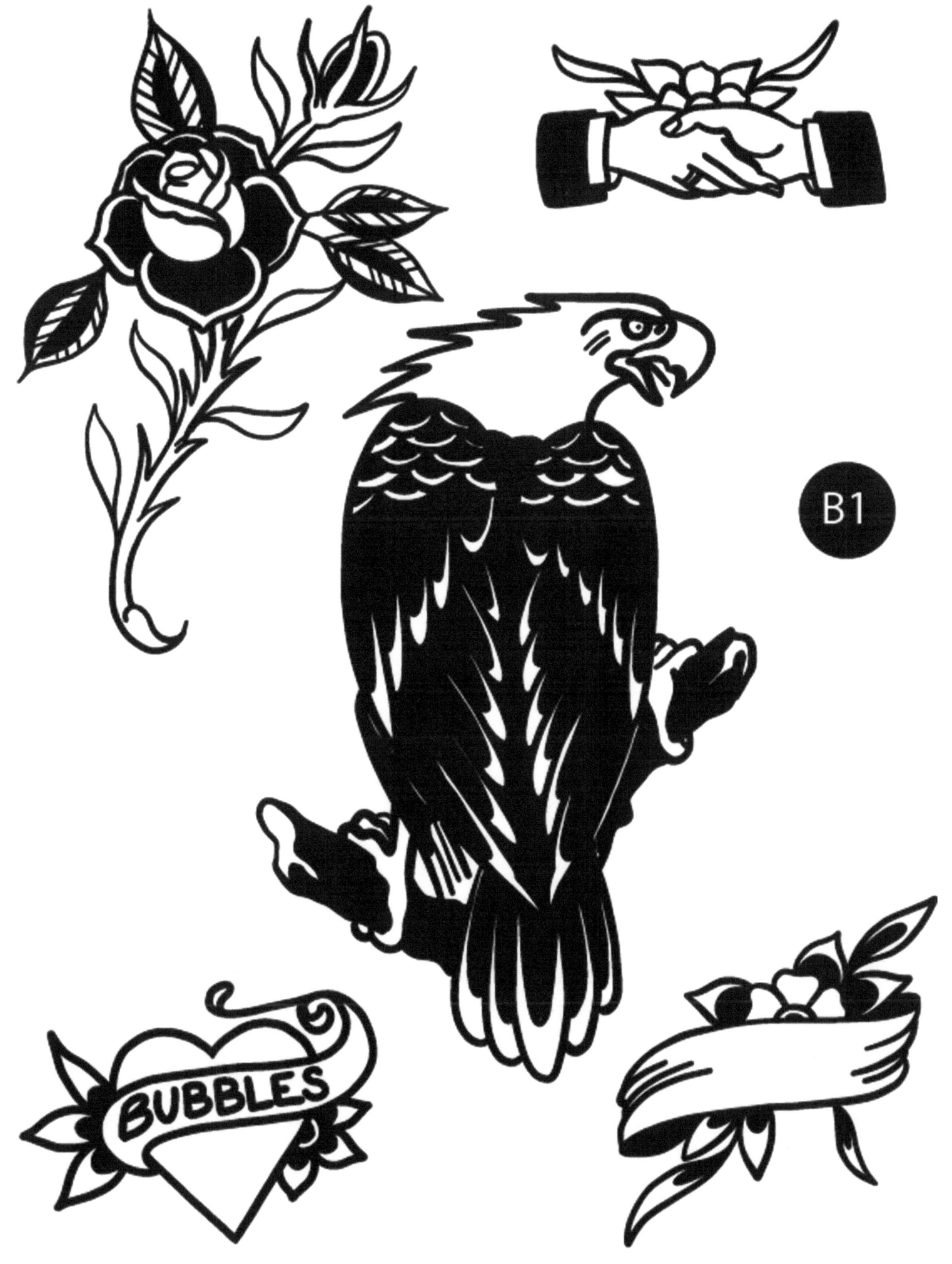

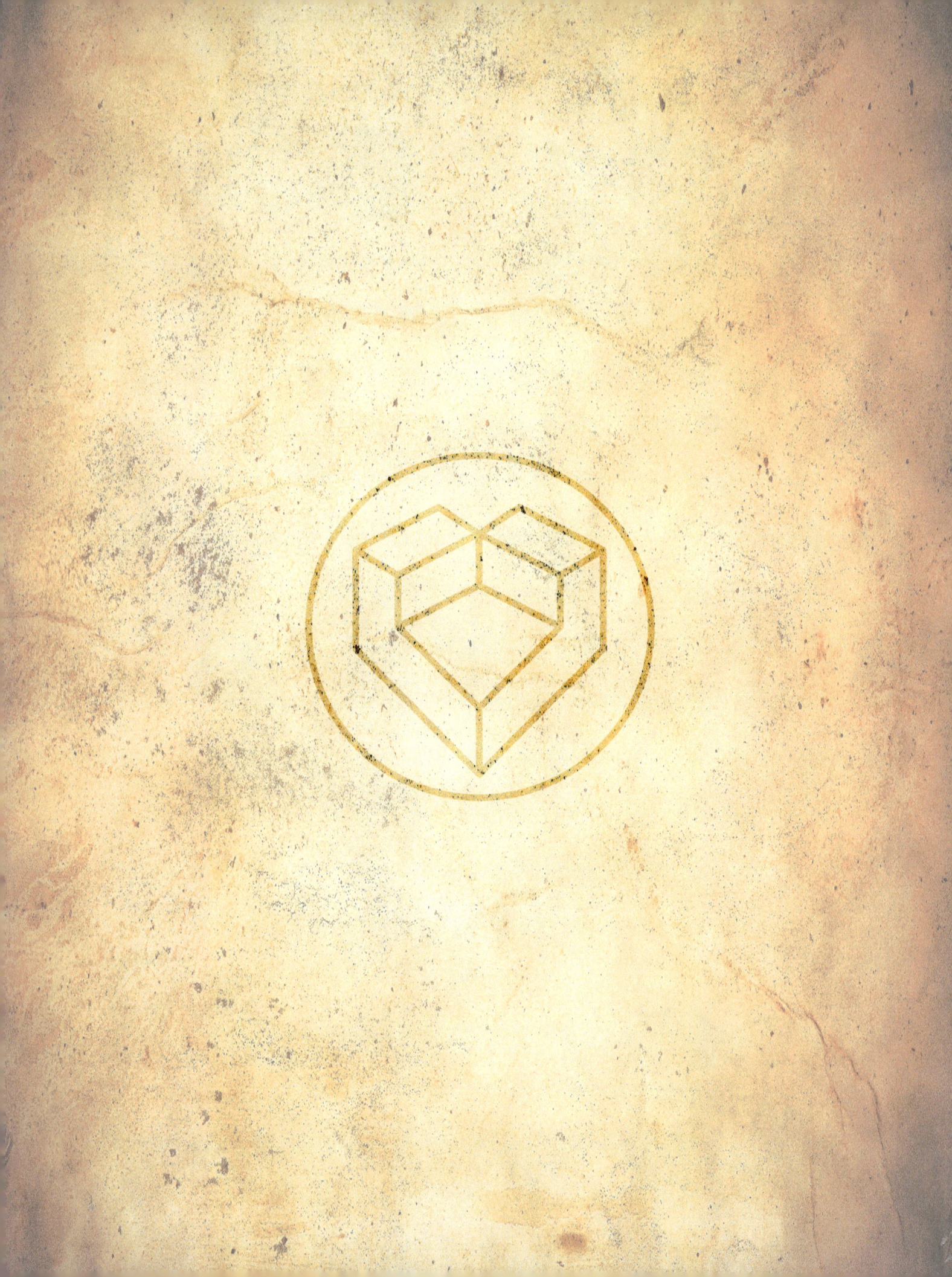

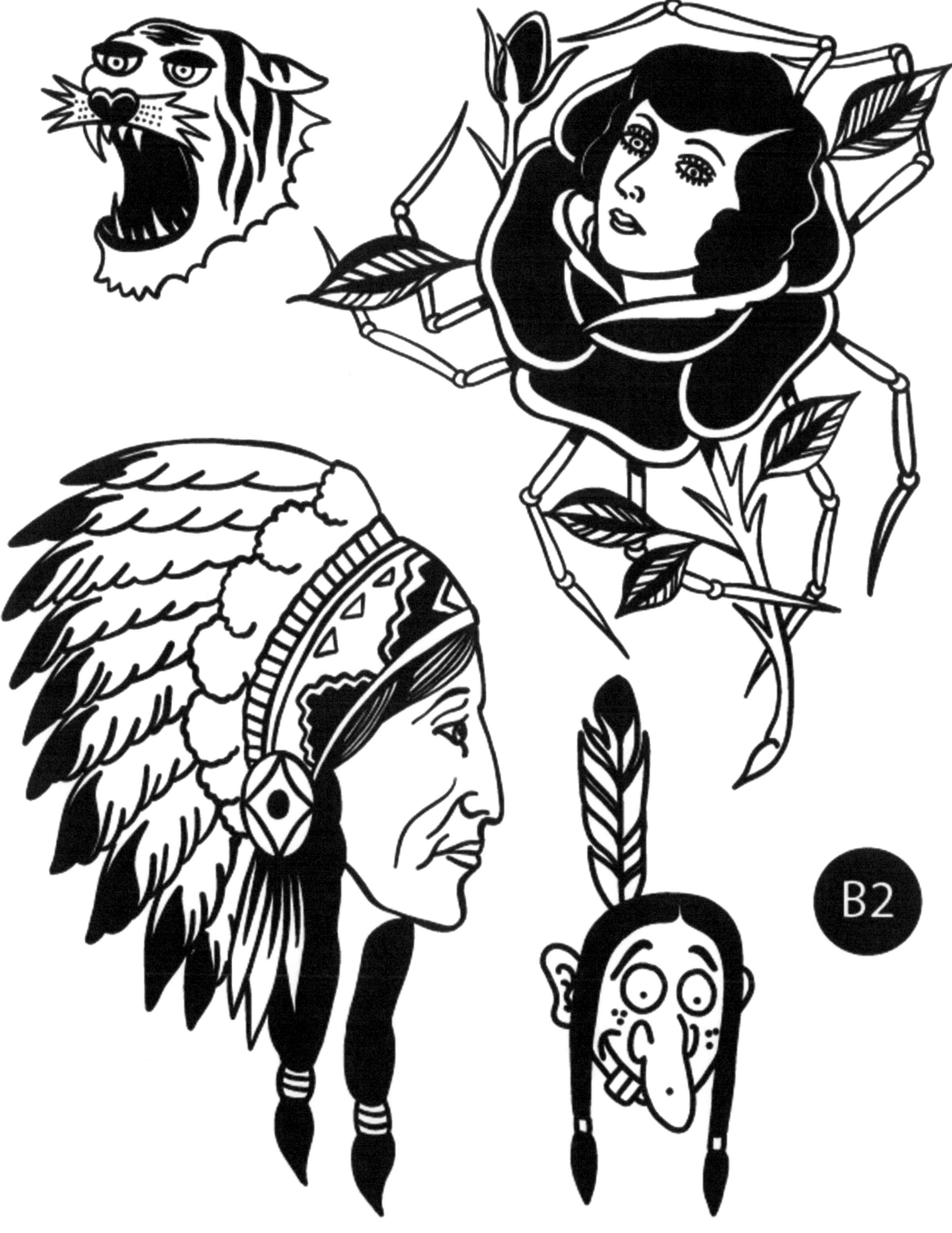

B2

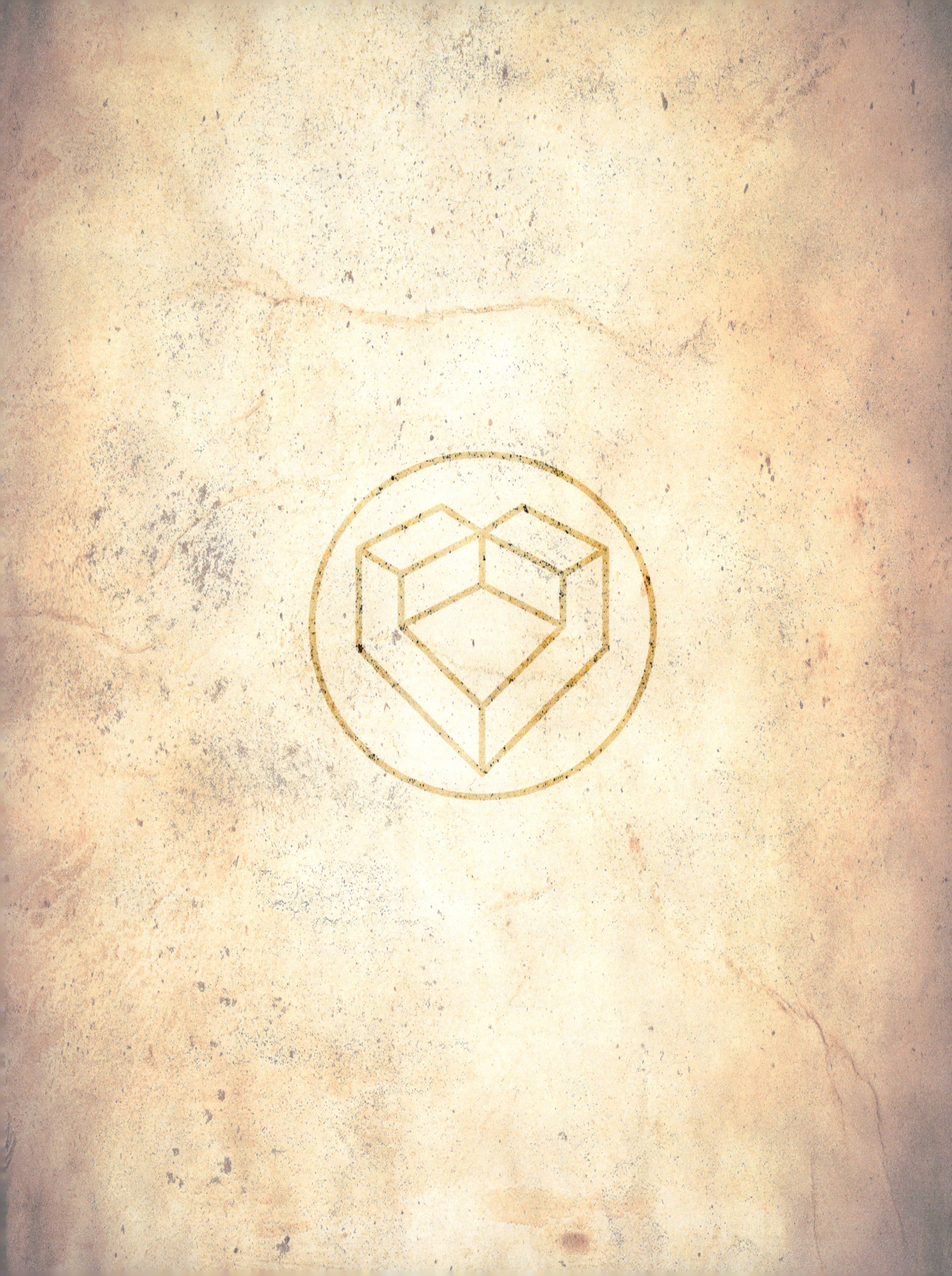

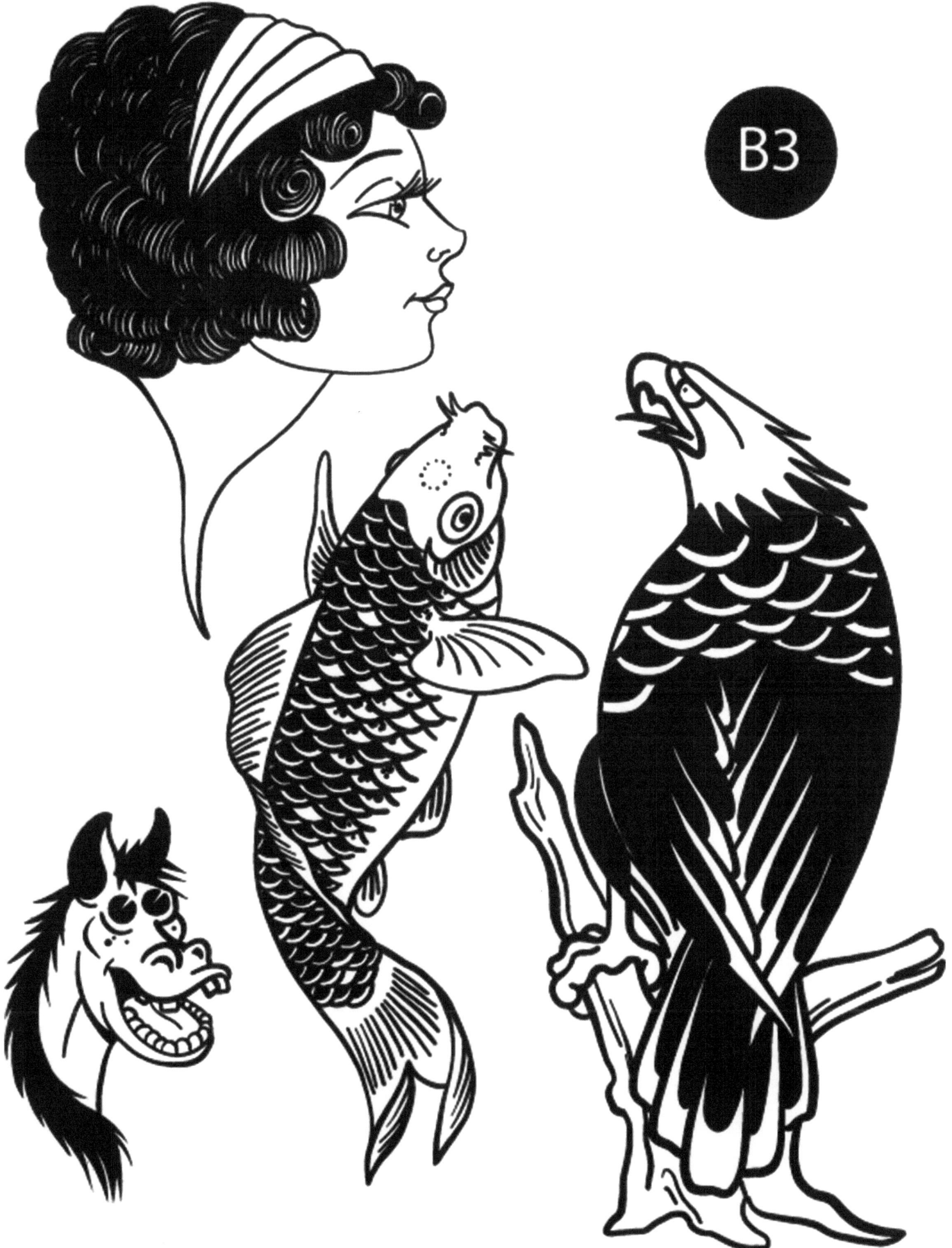

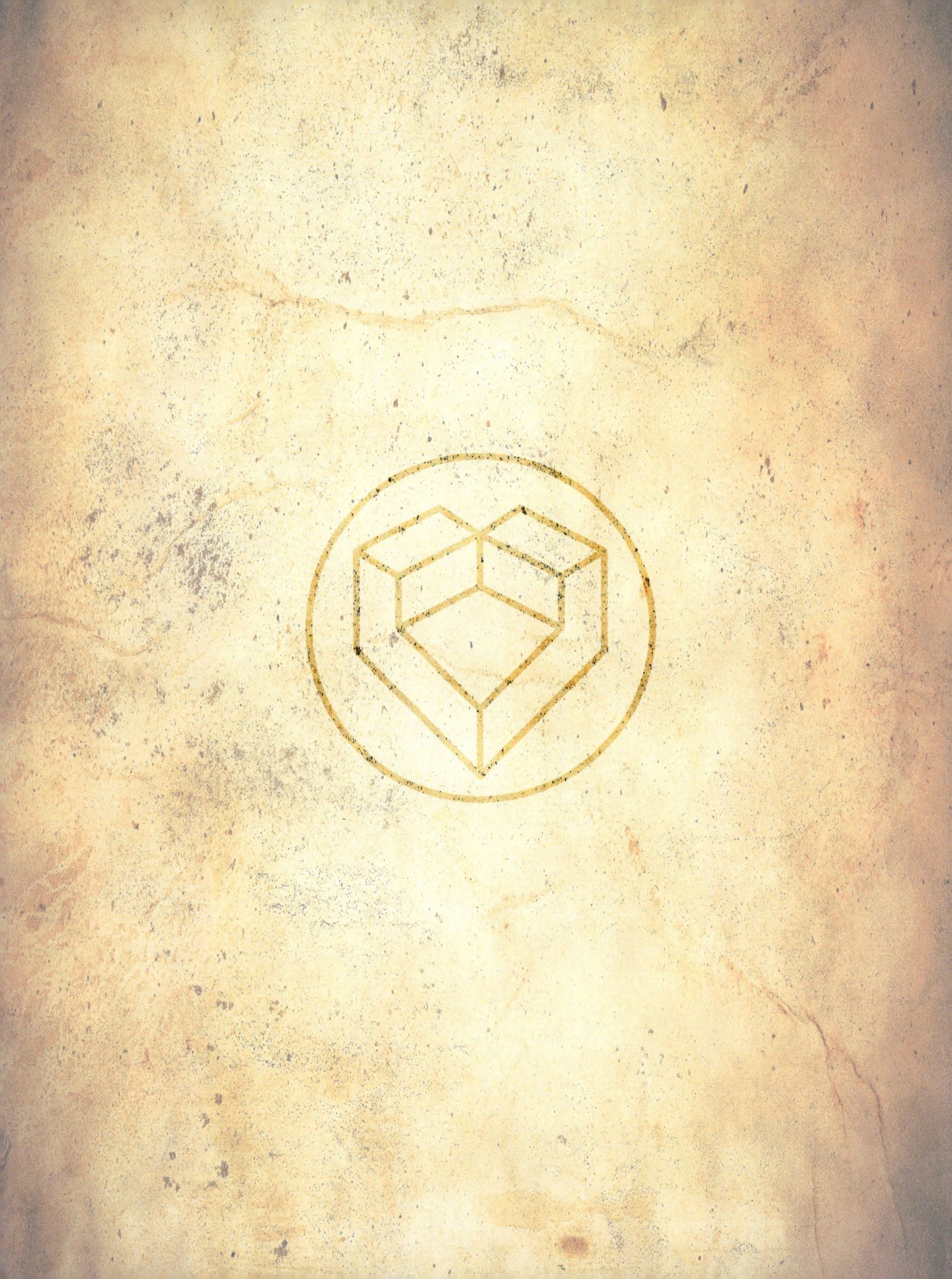

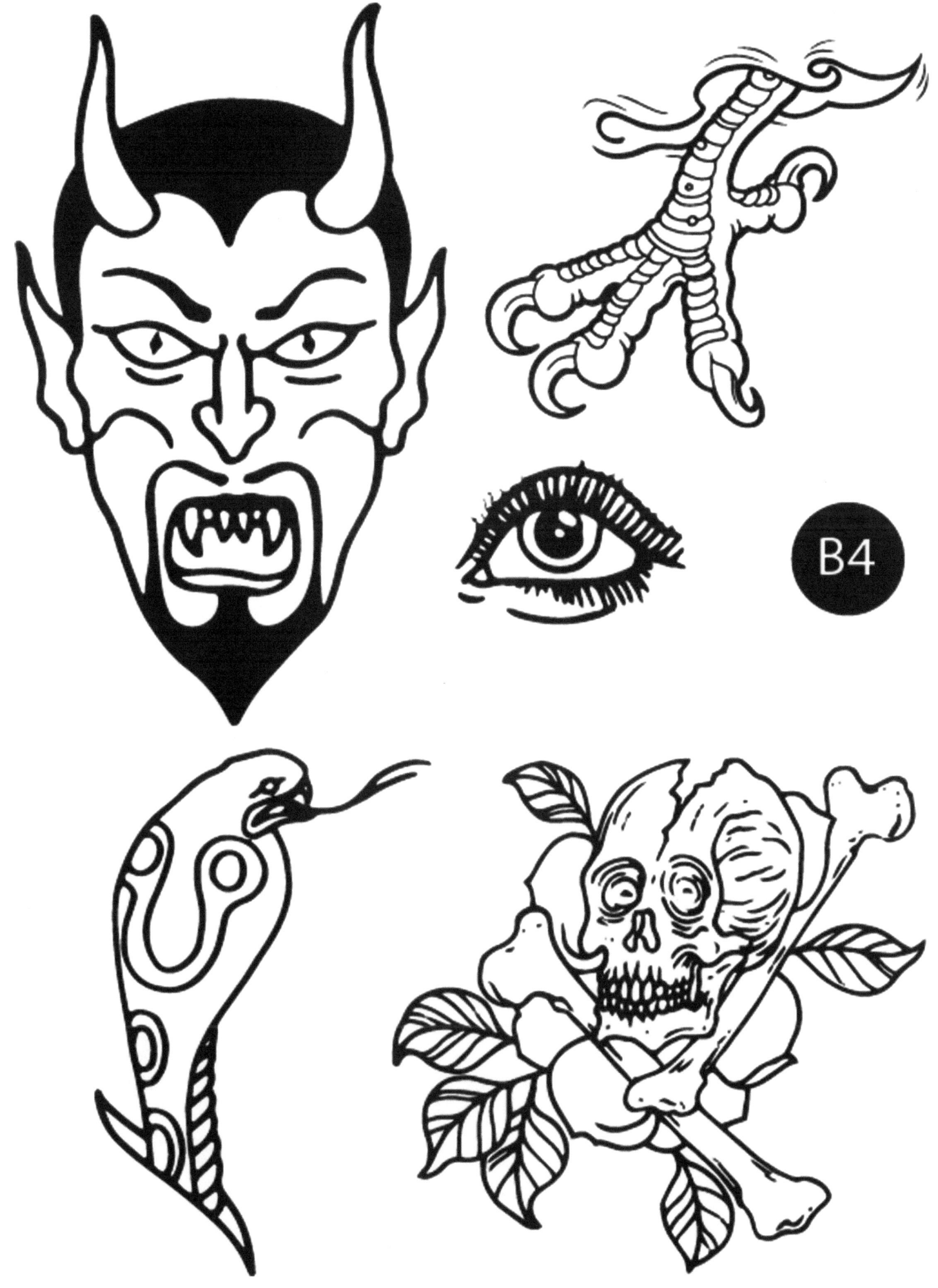

B4

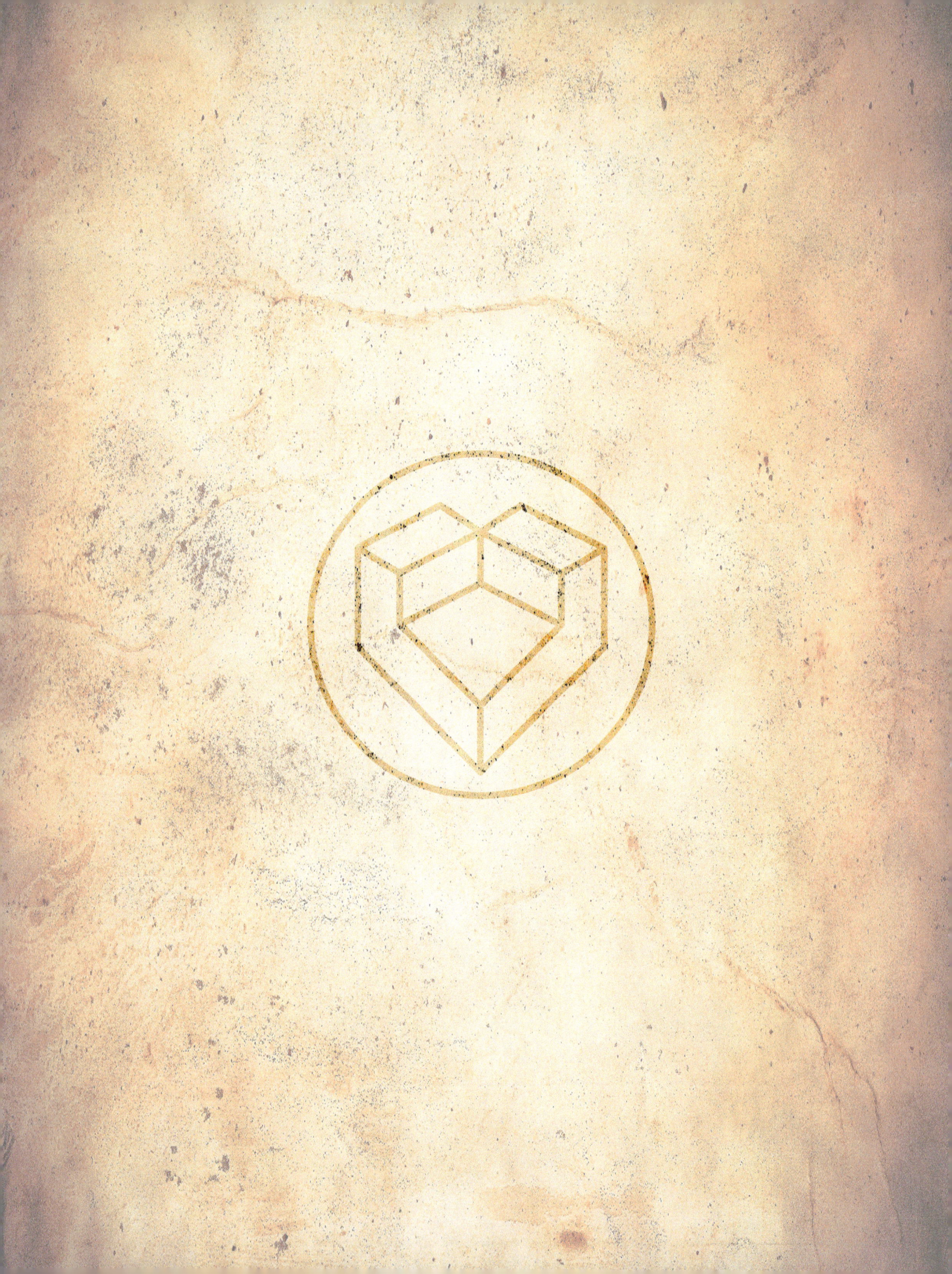

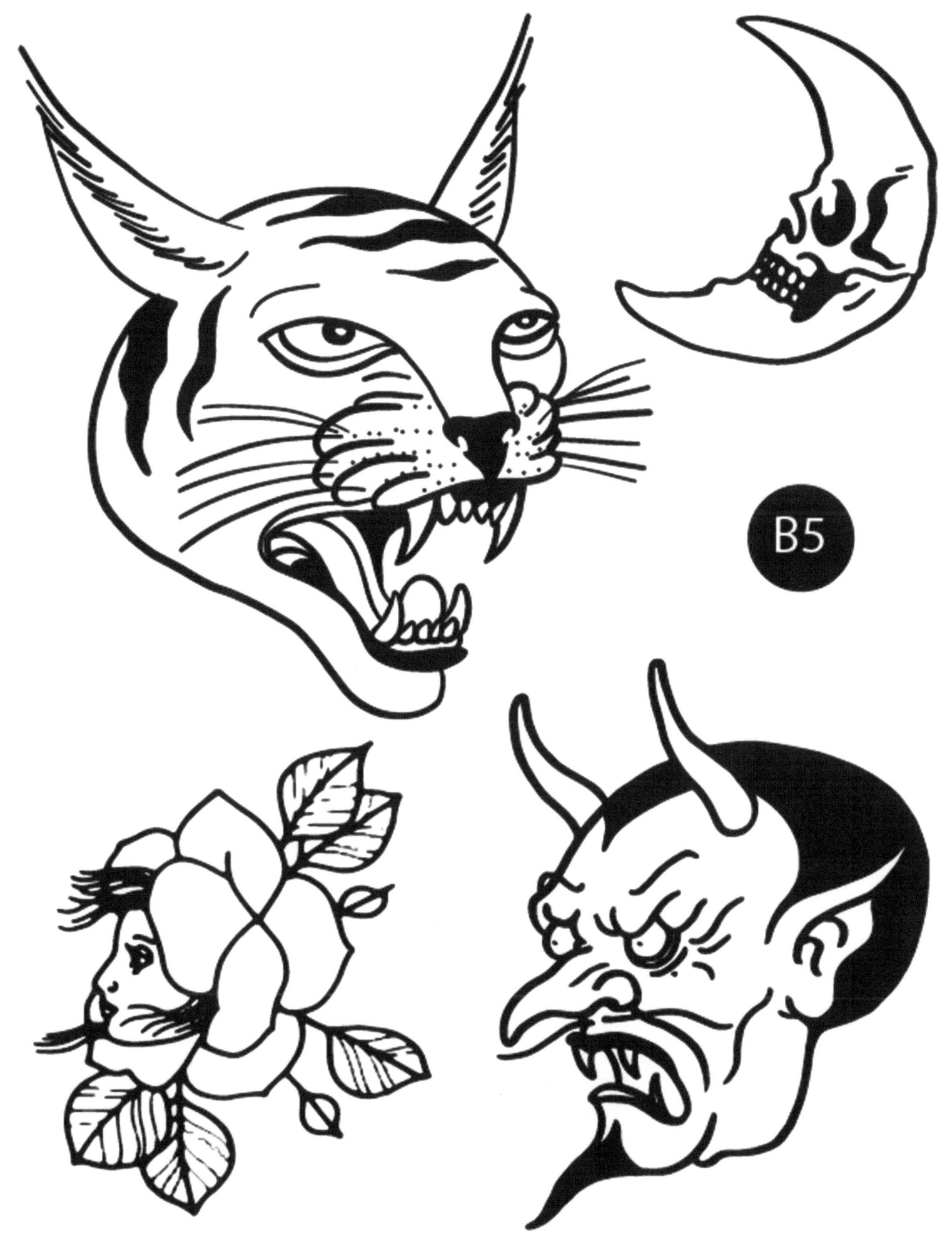

B5

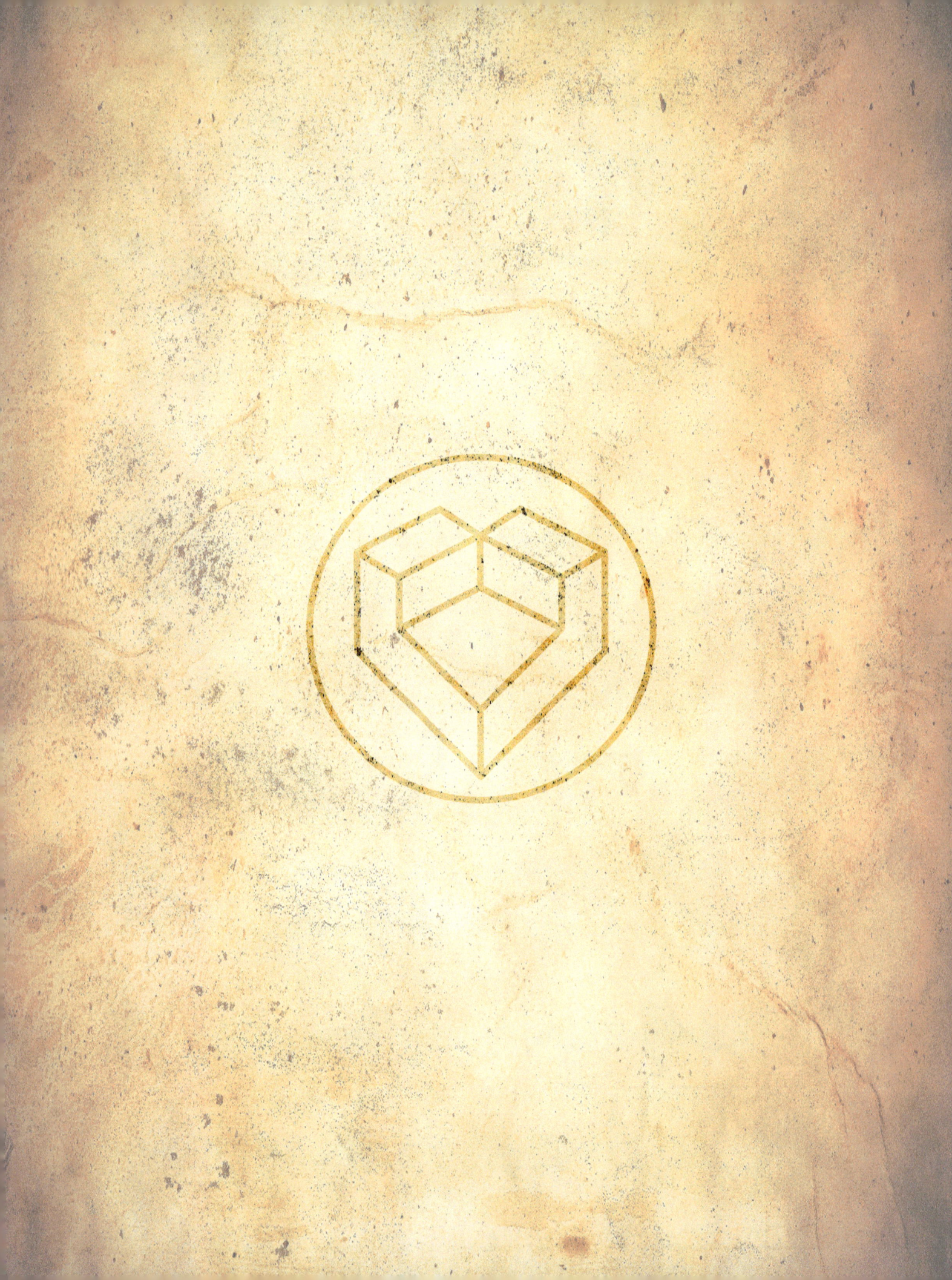

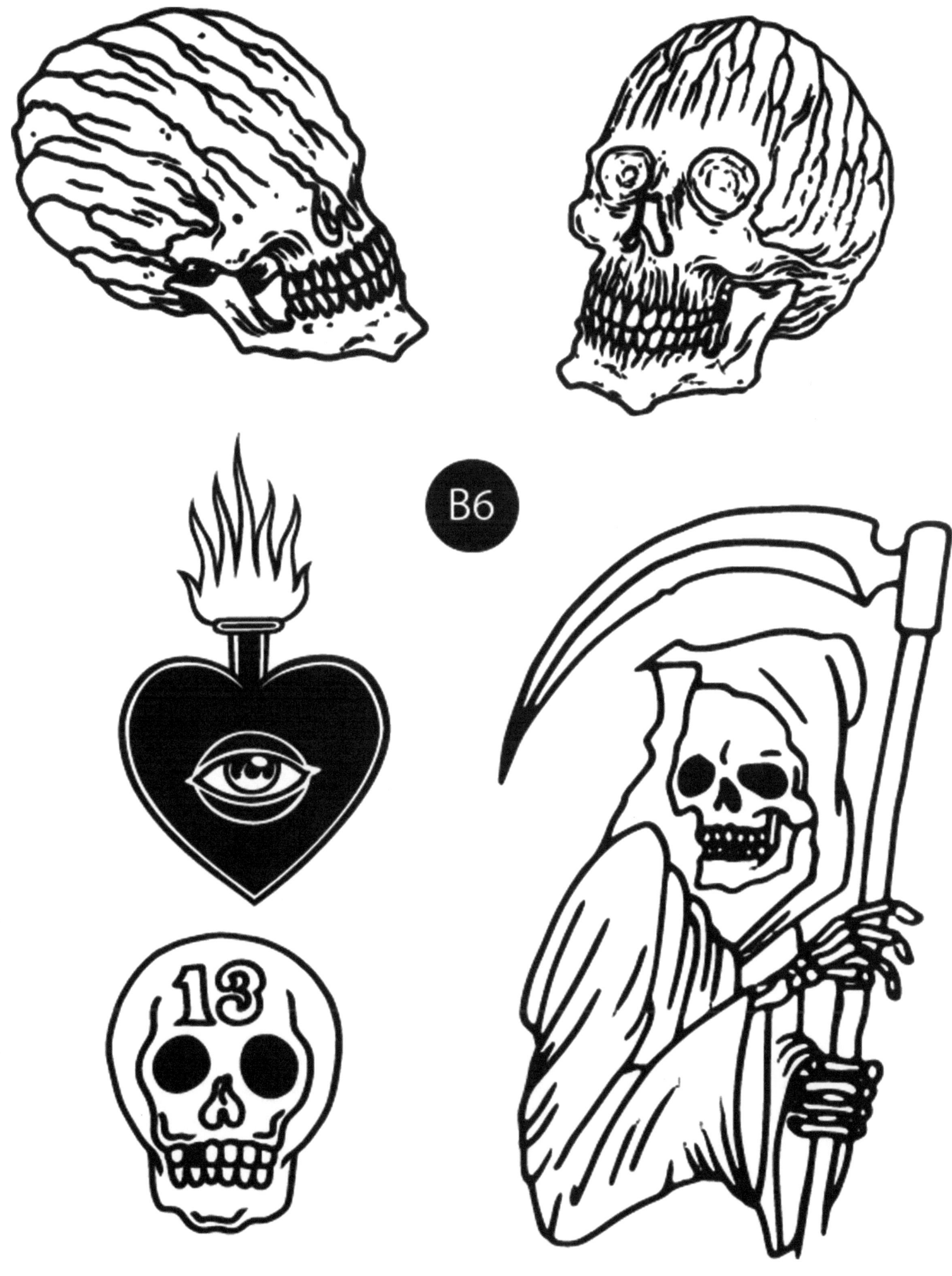

B6

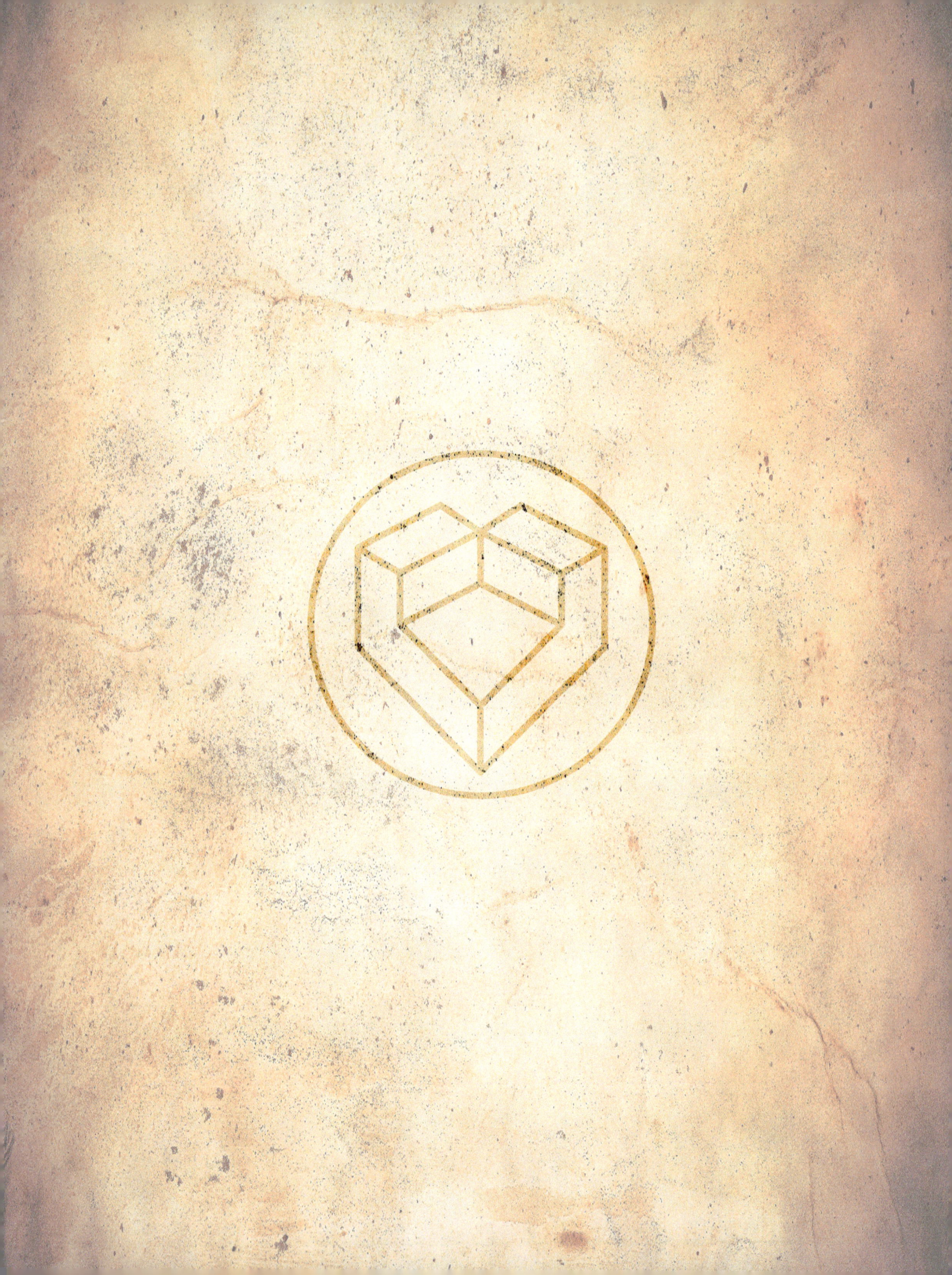

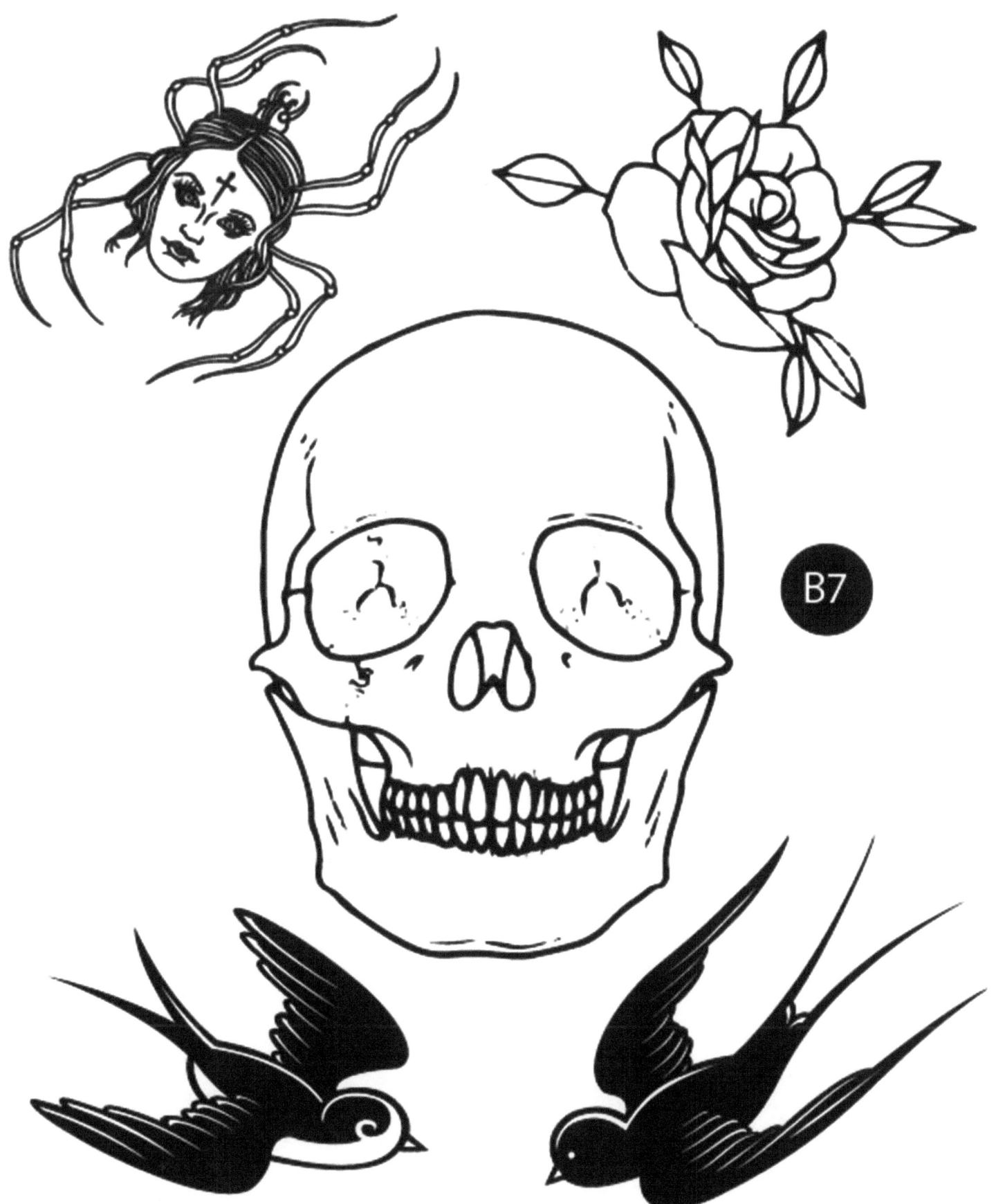

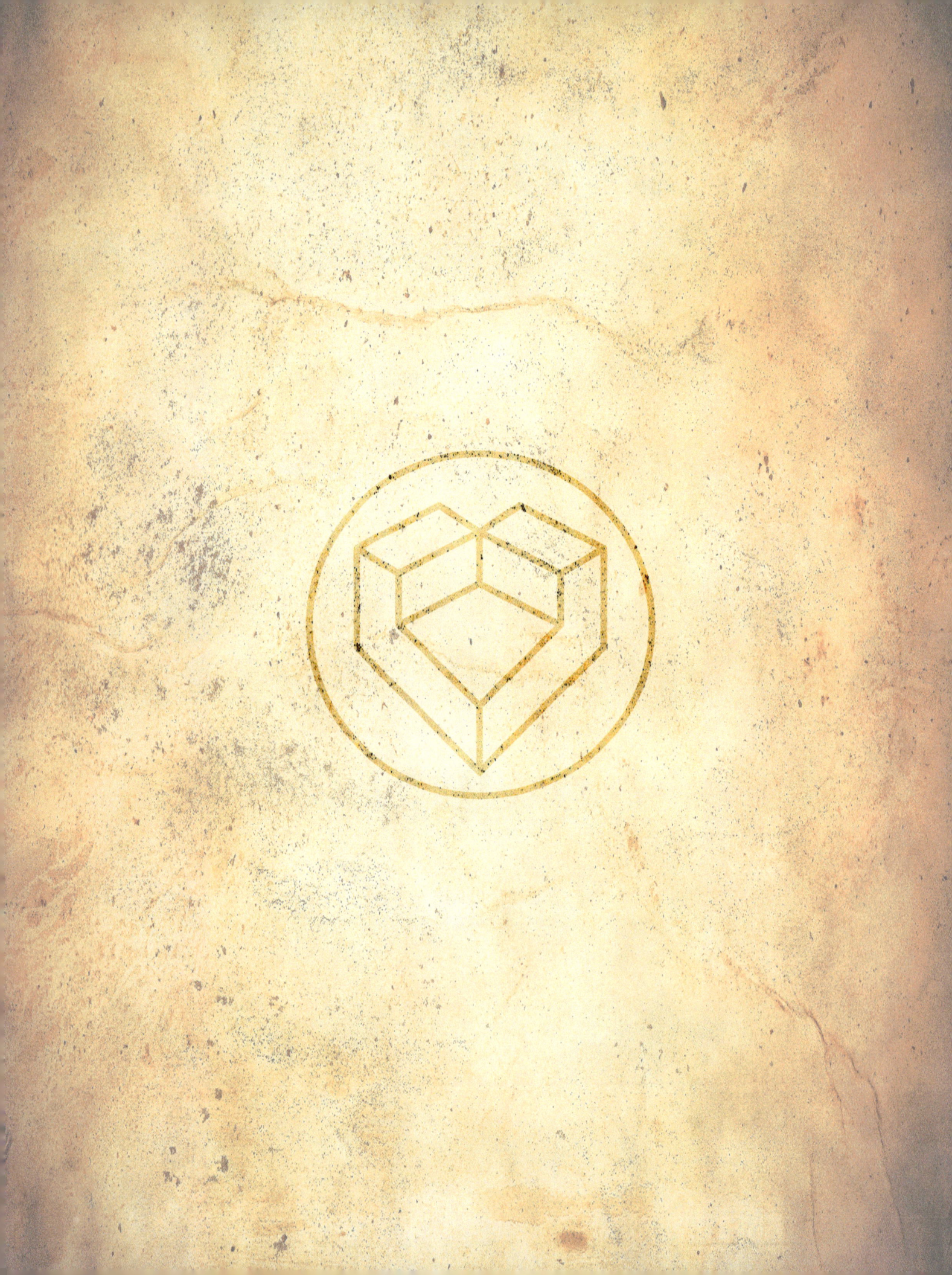

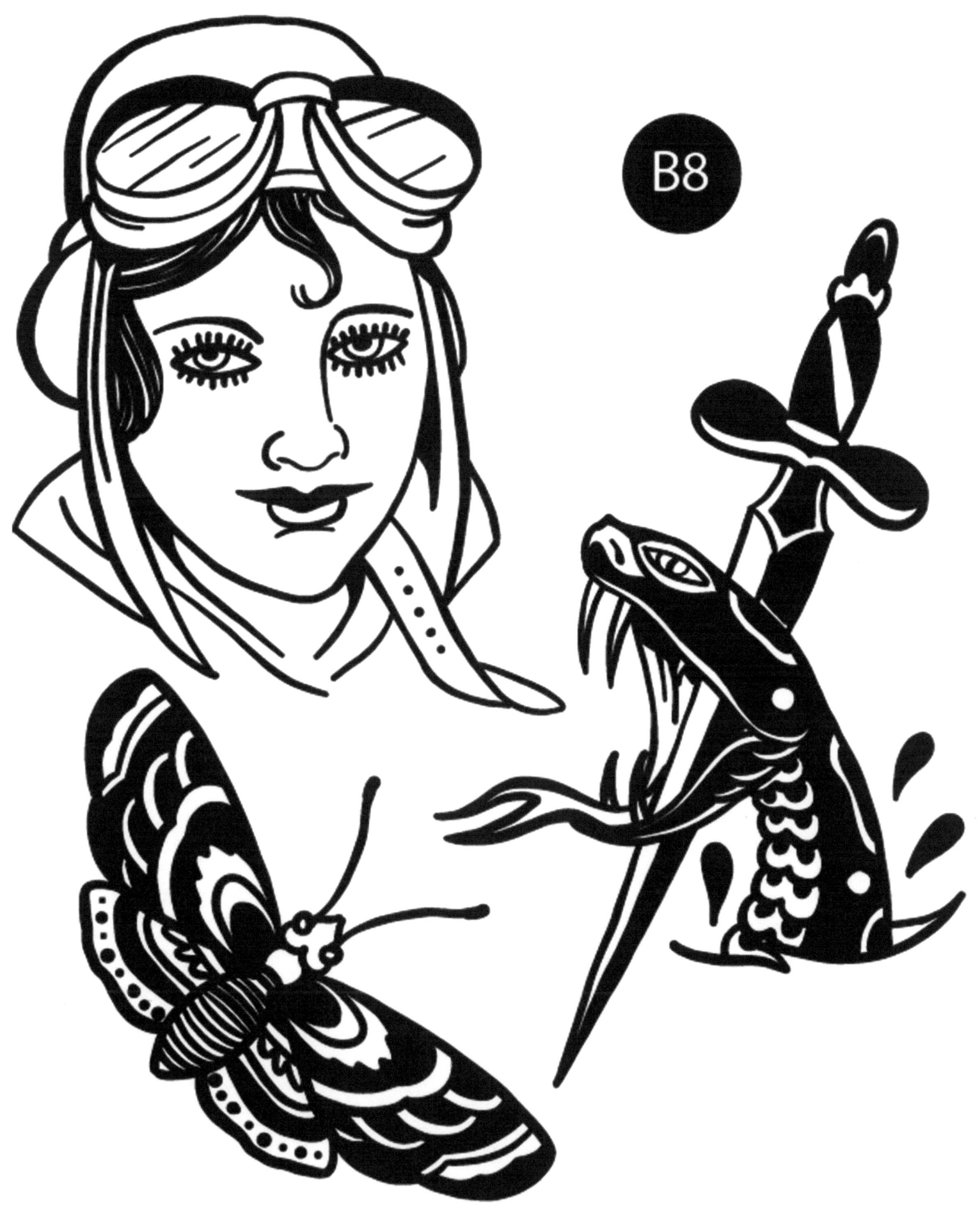

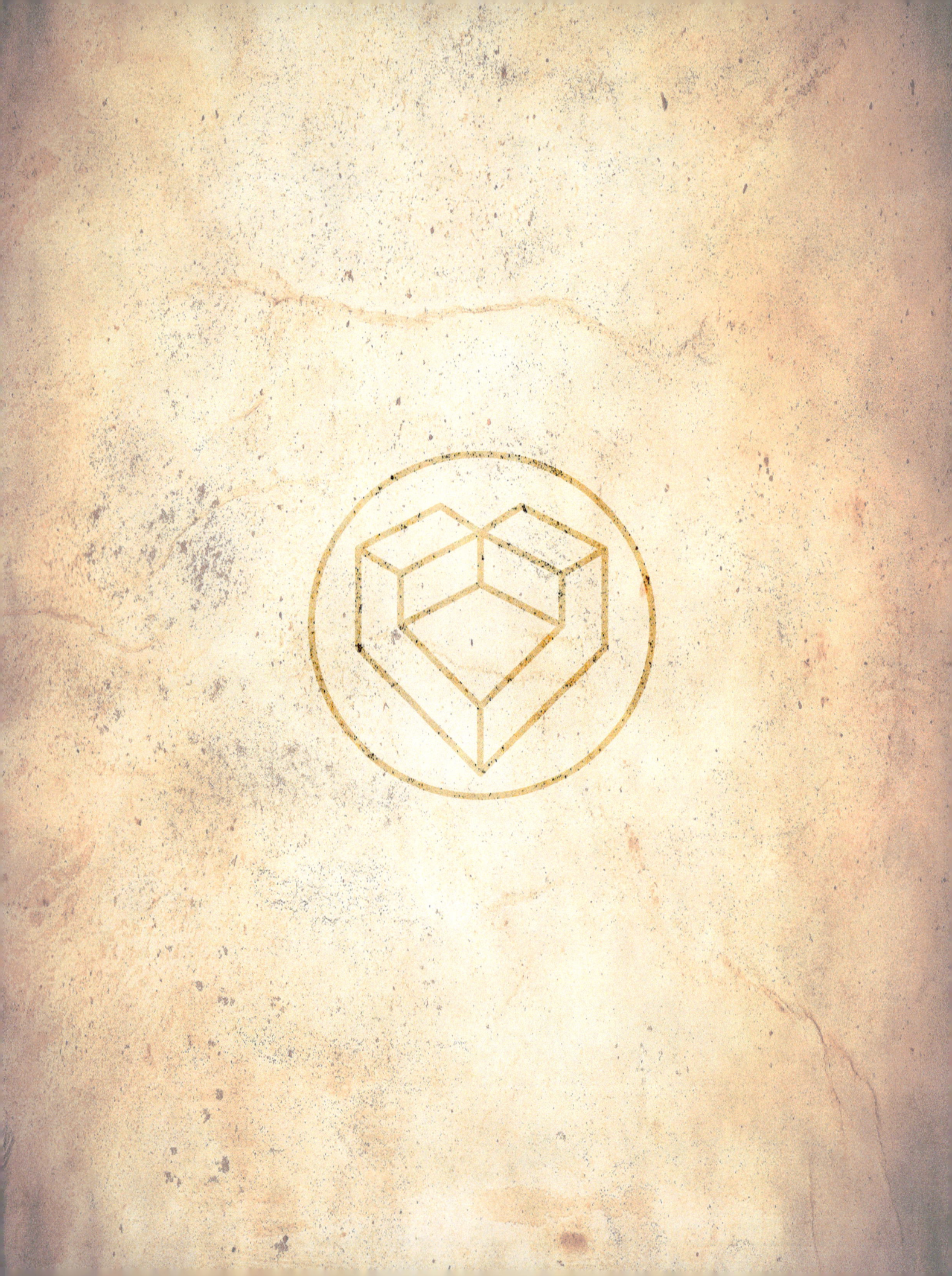

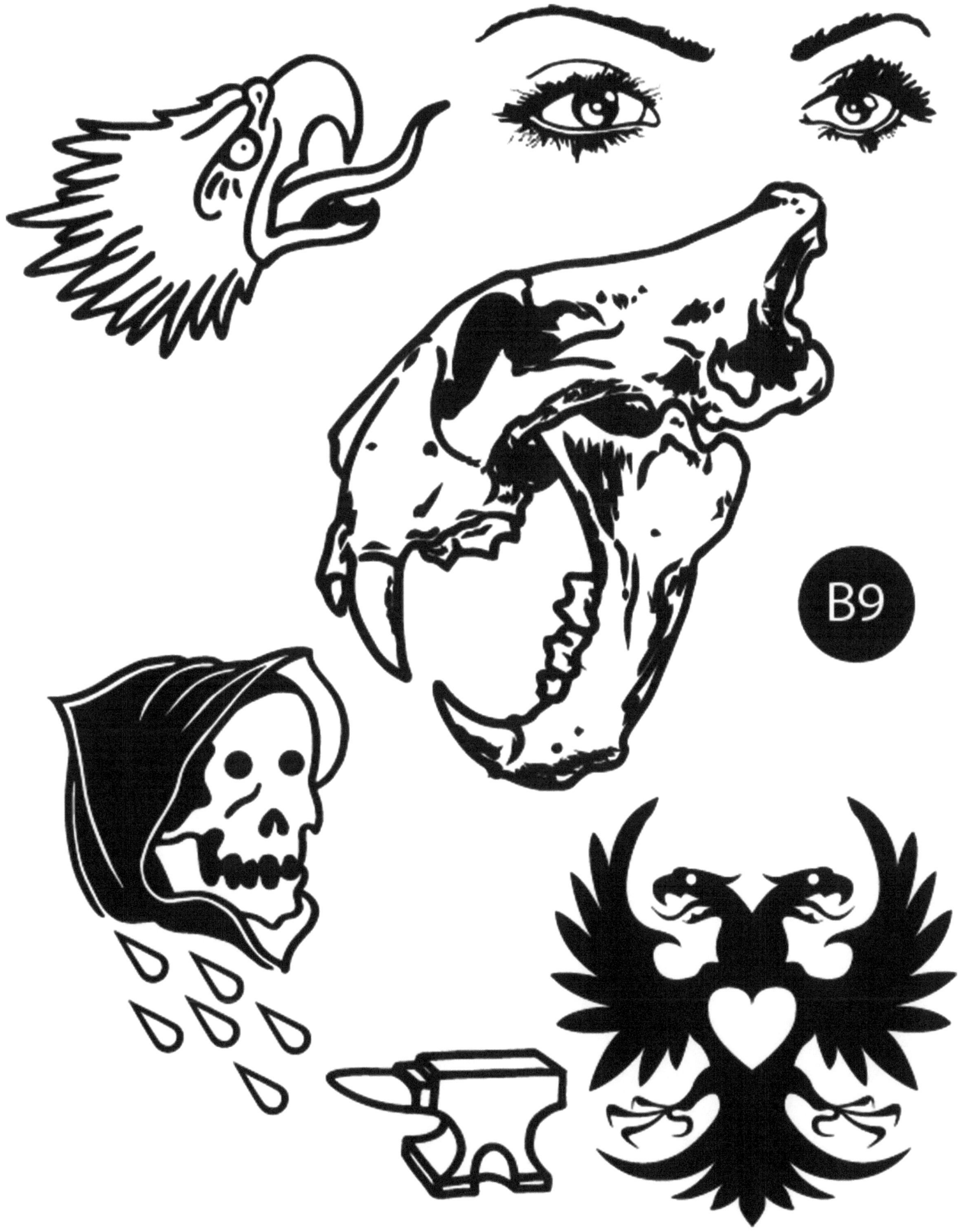

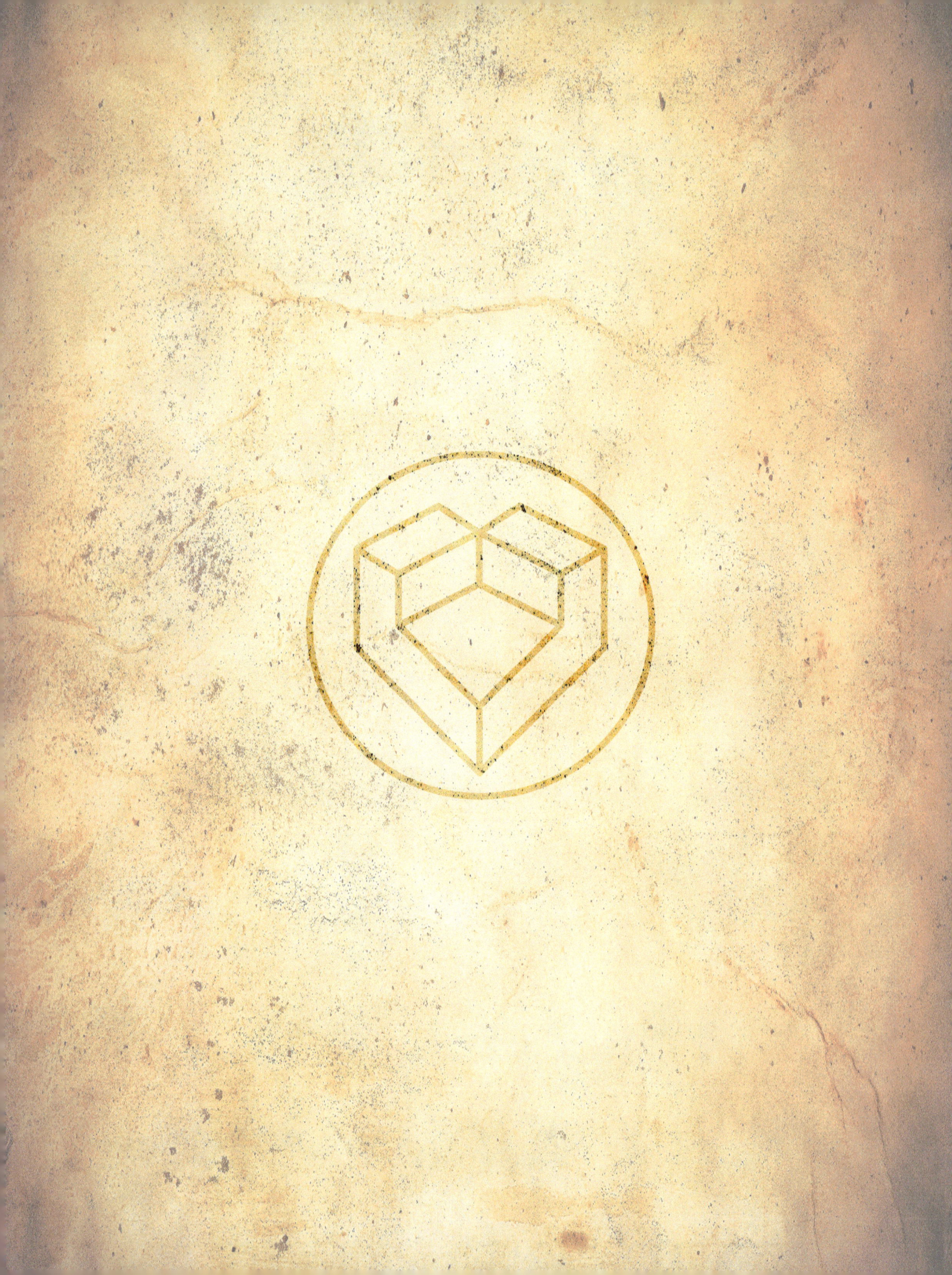

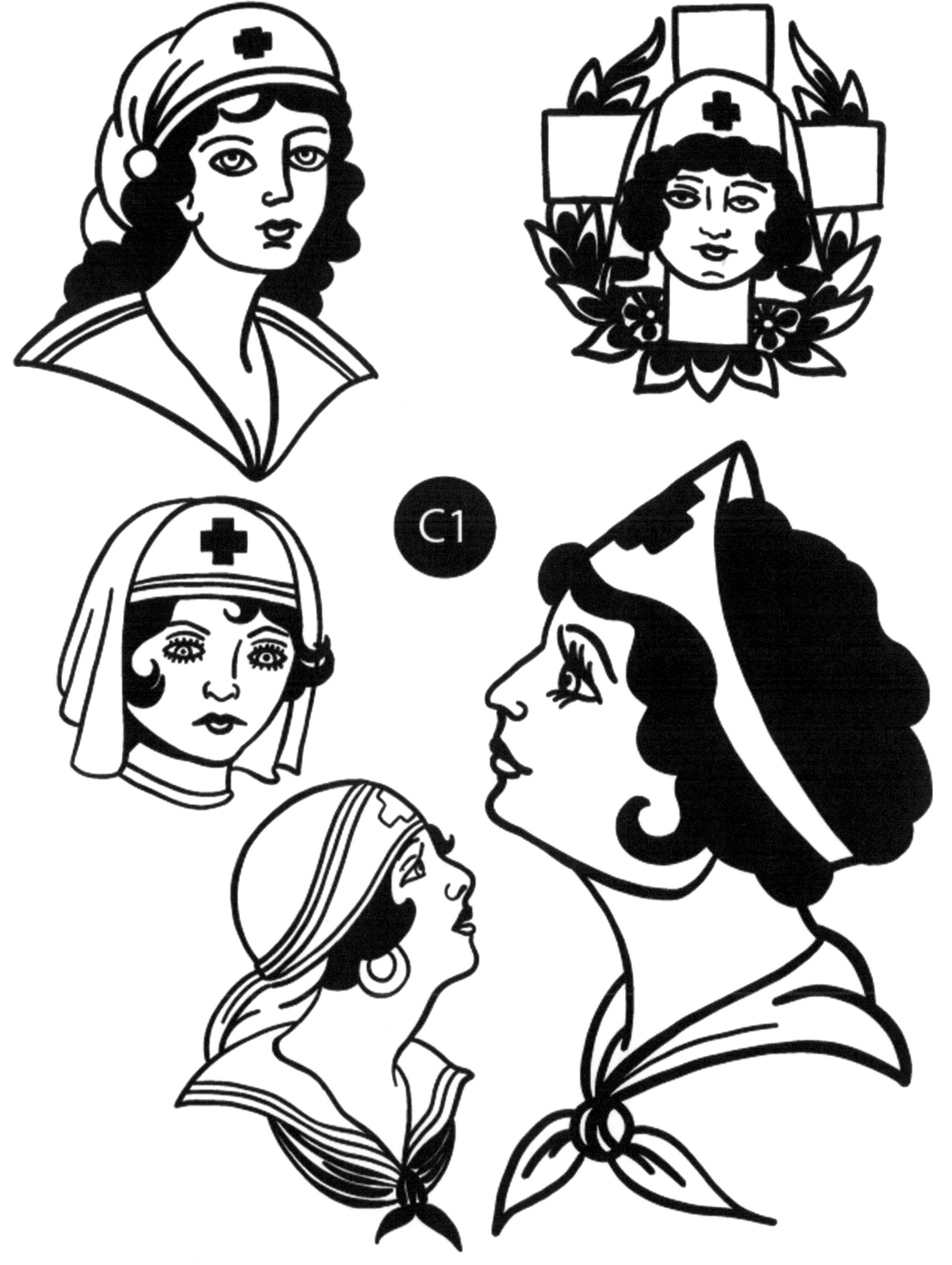

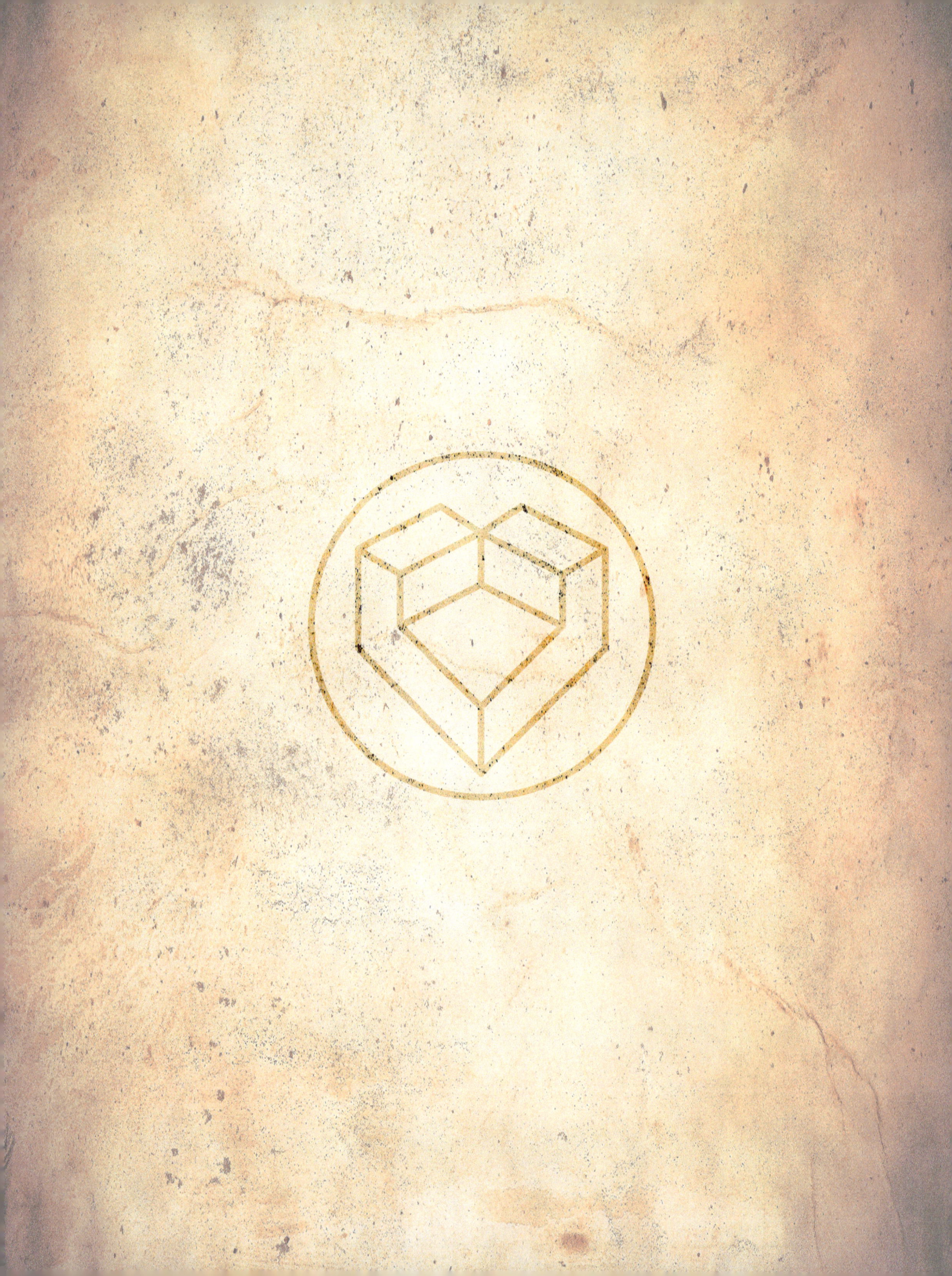

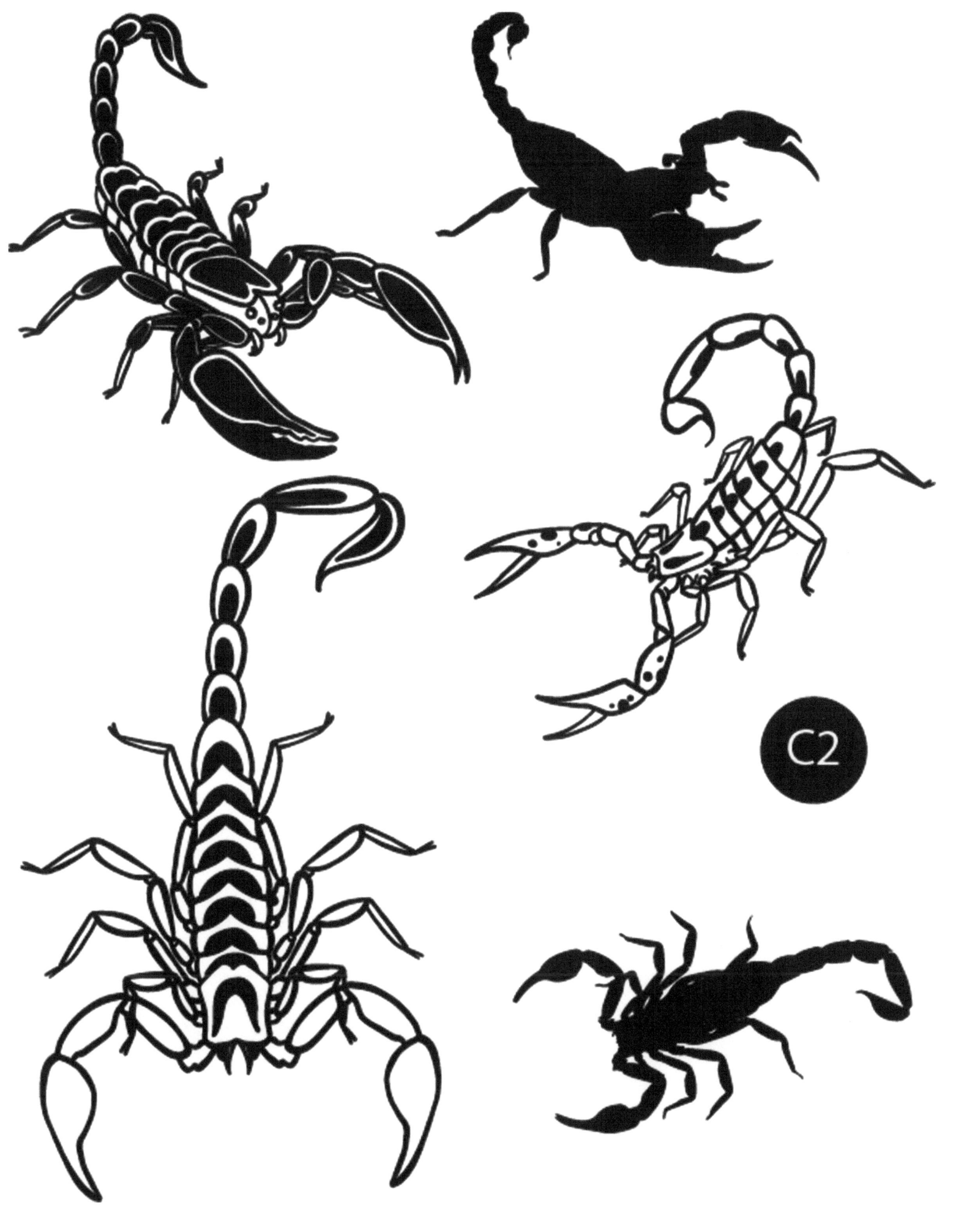

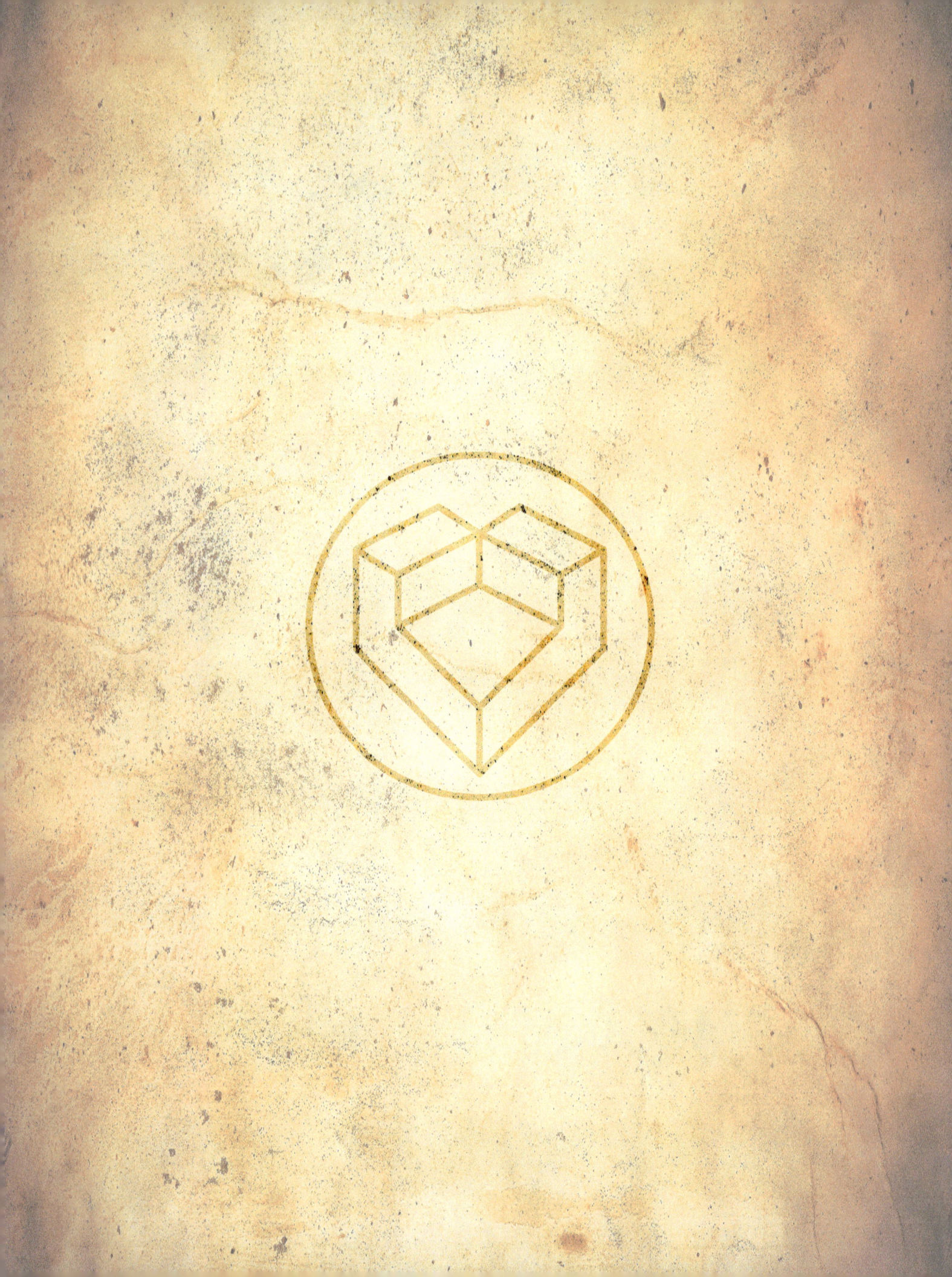

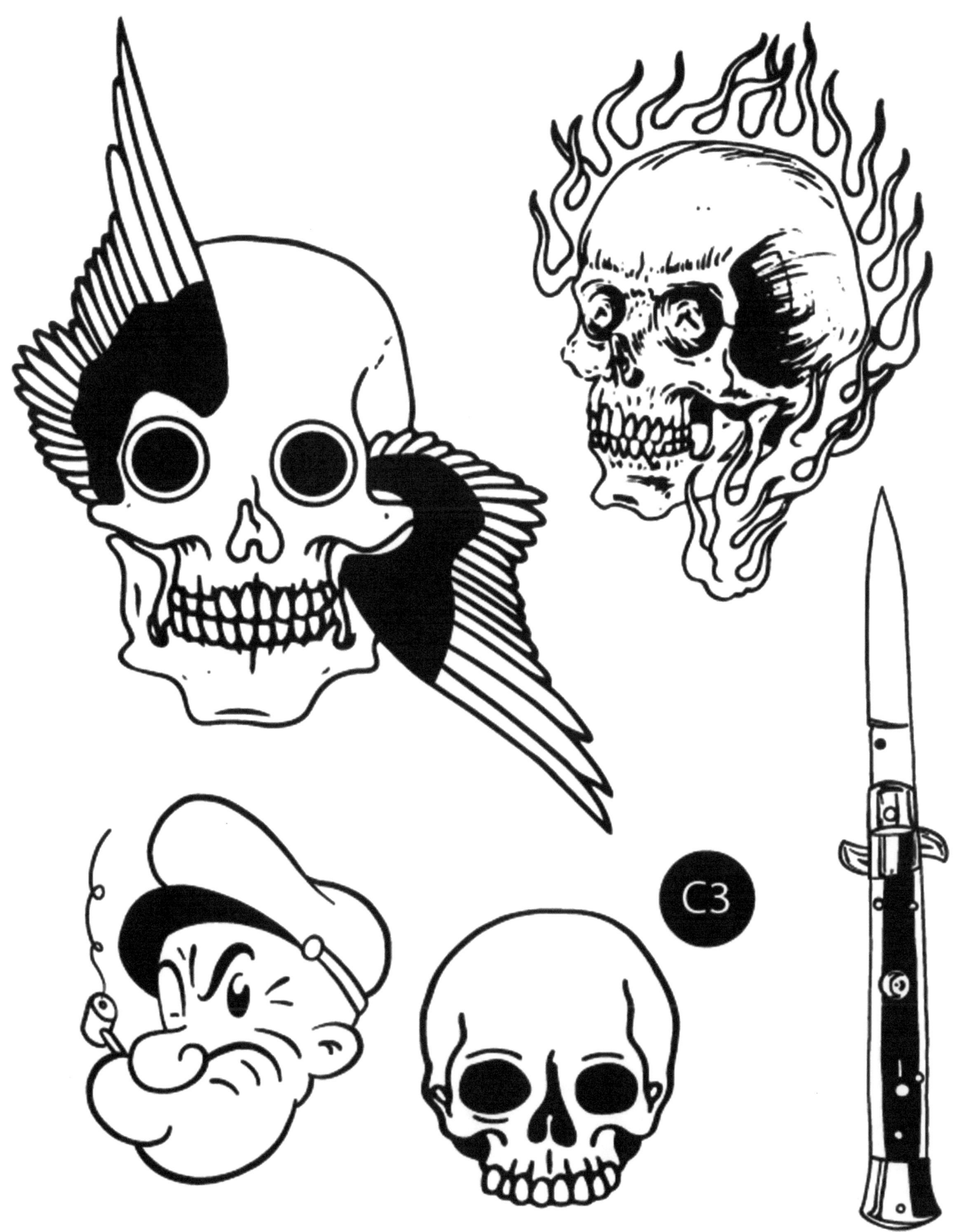

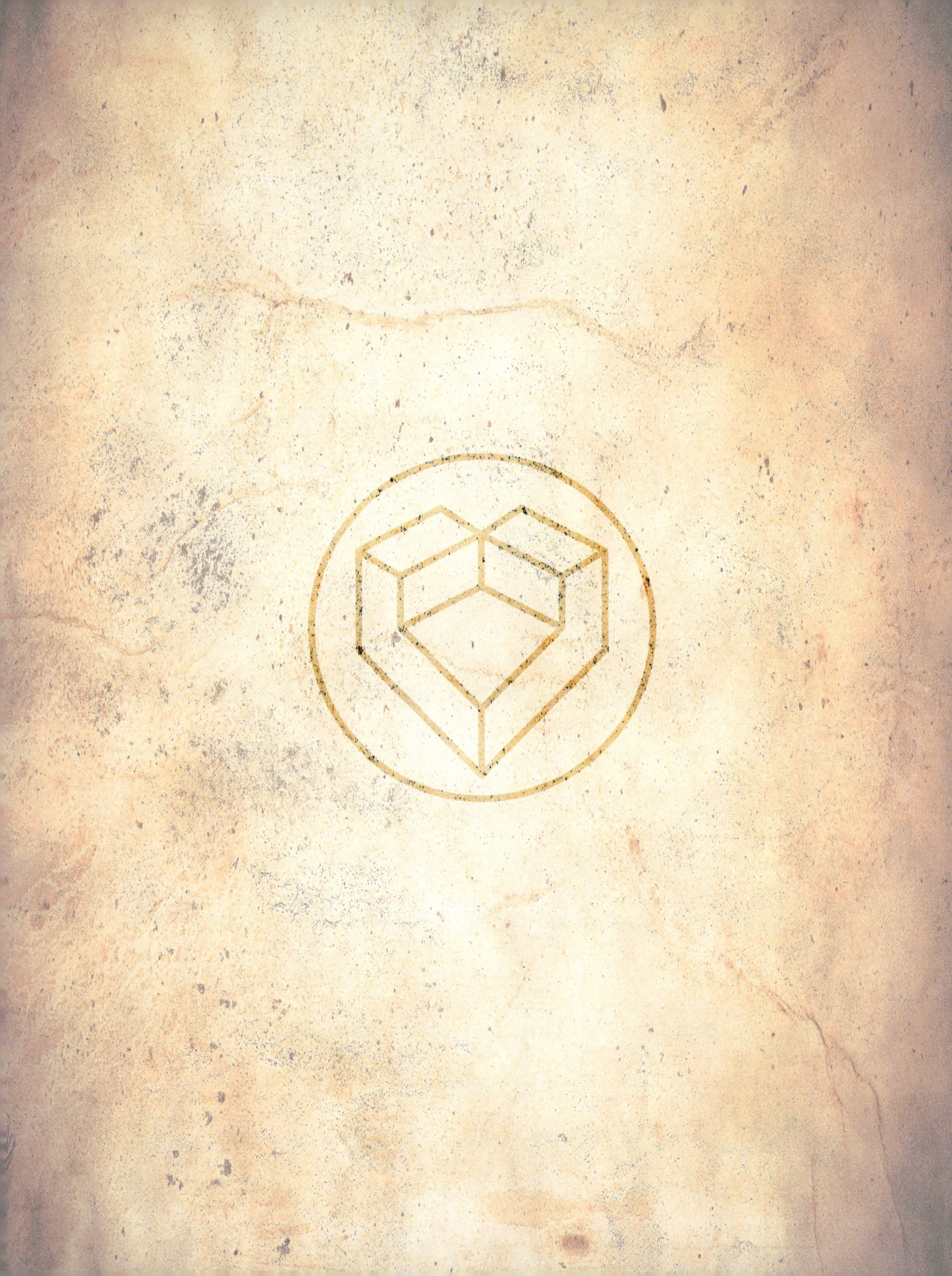

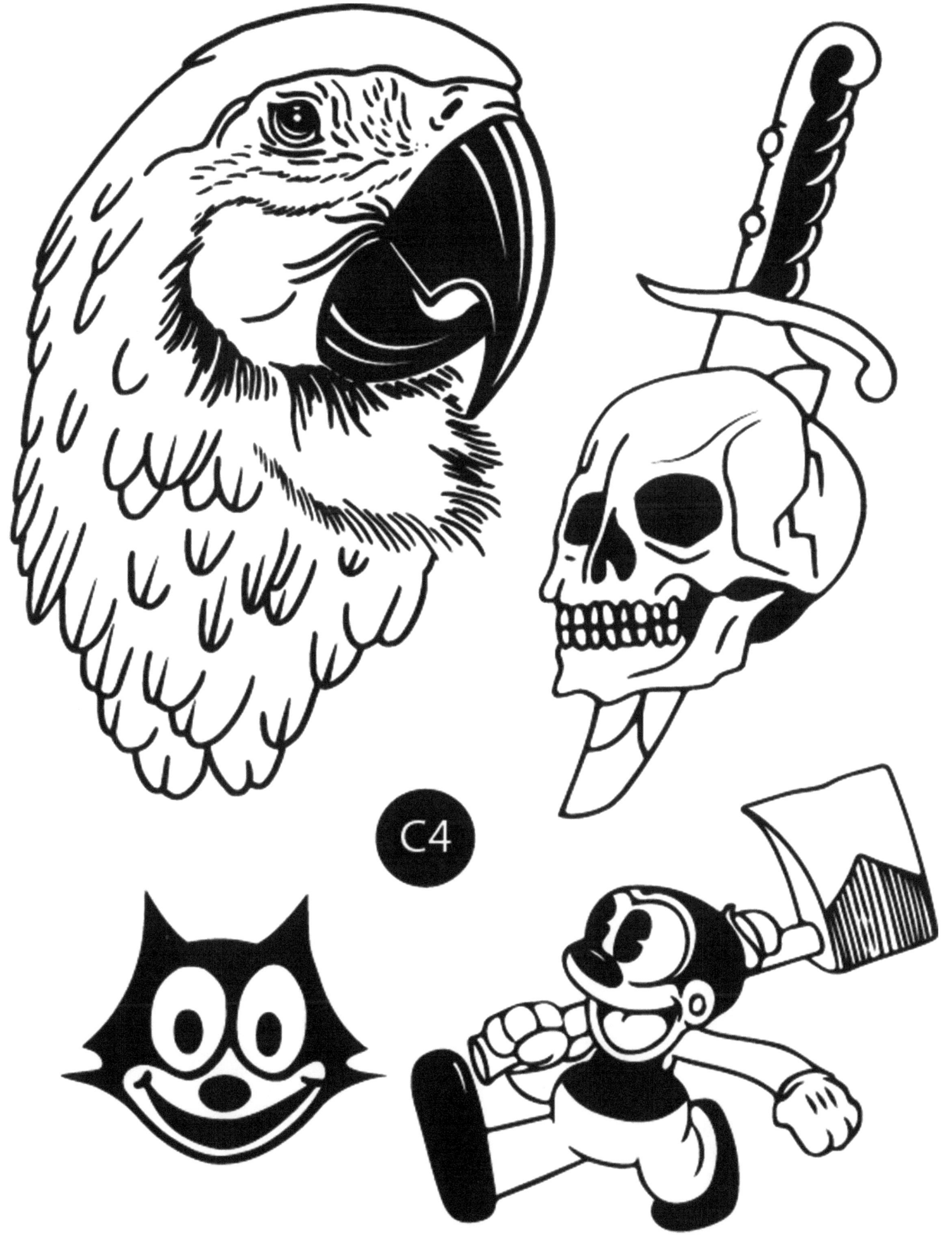

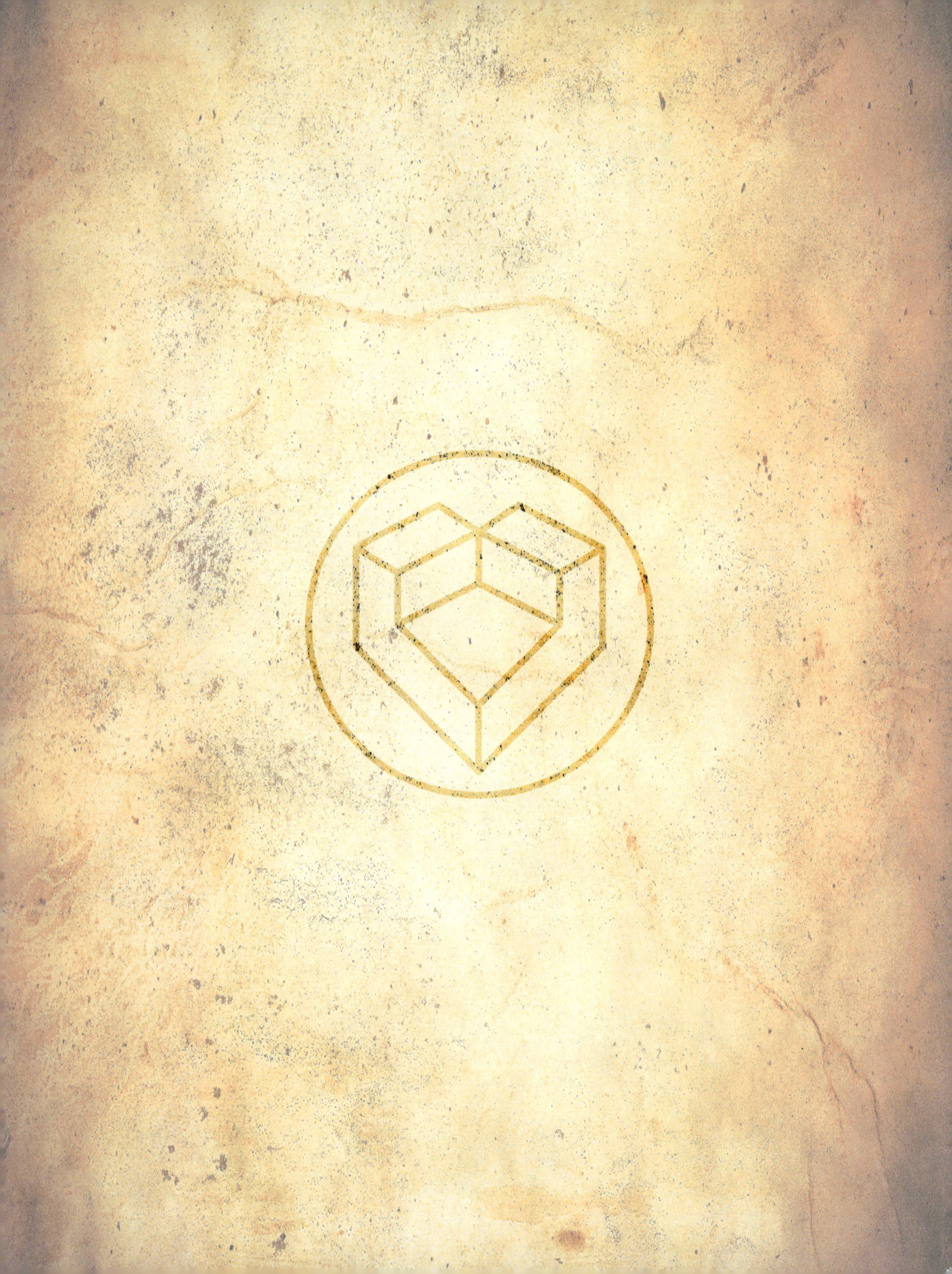

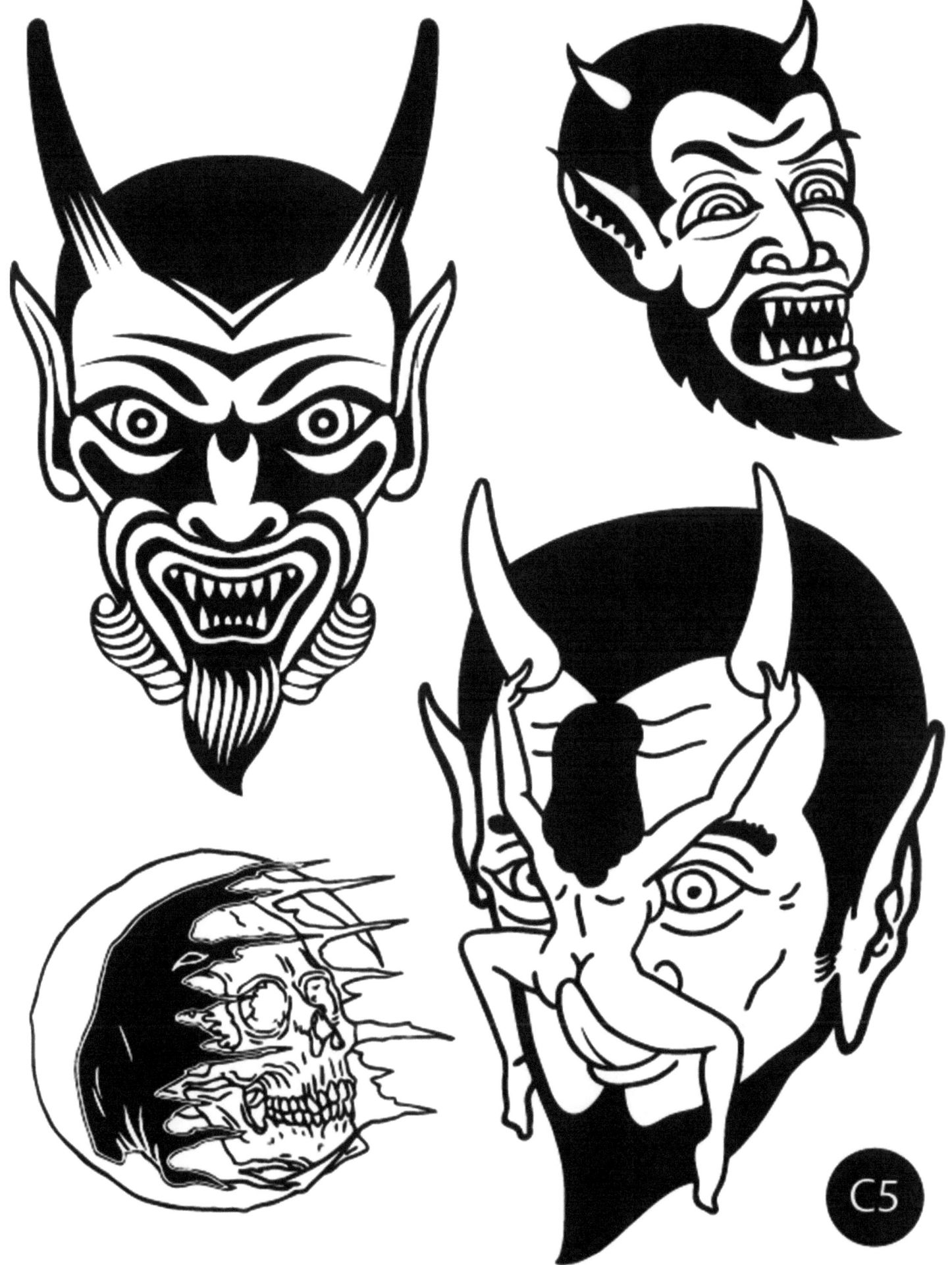

C5

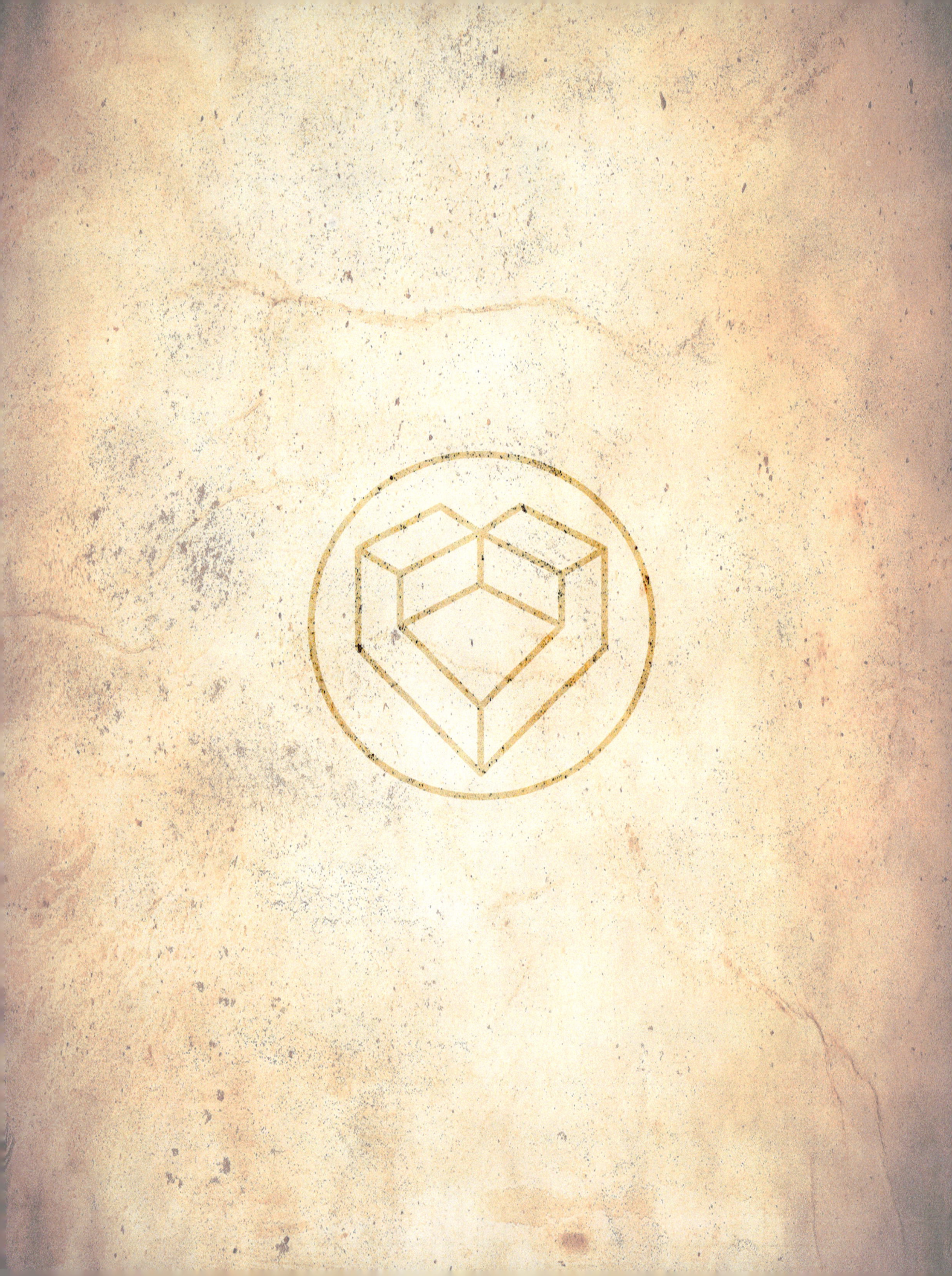

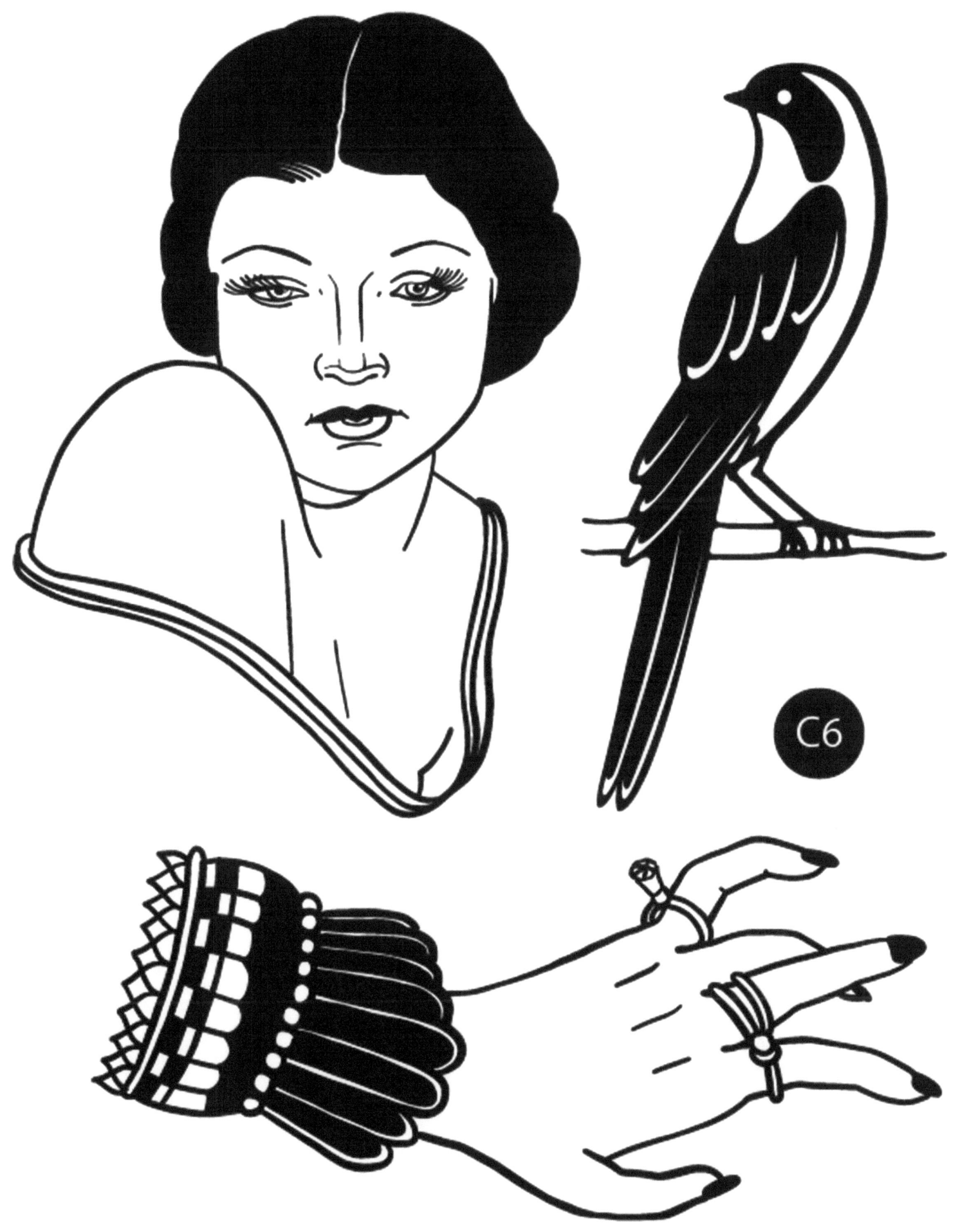

C6

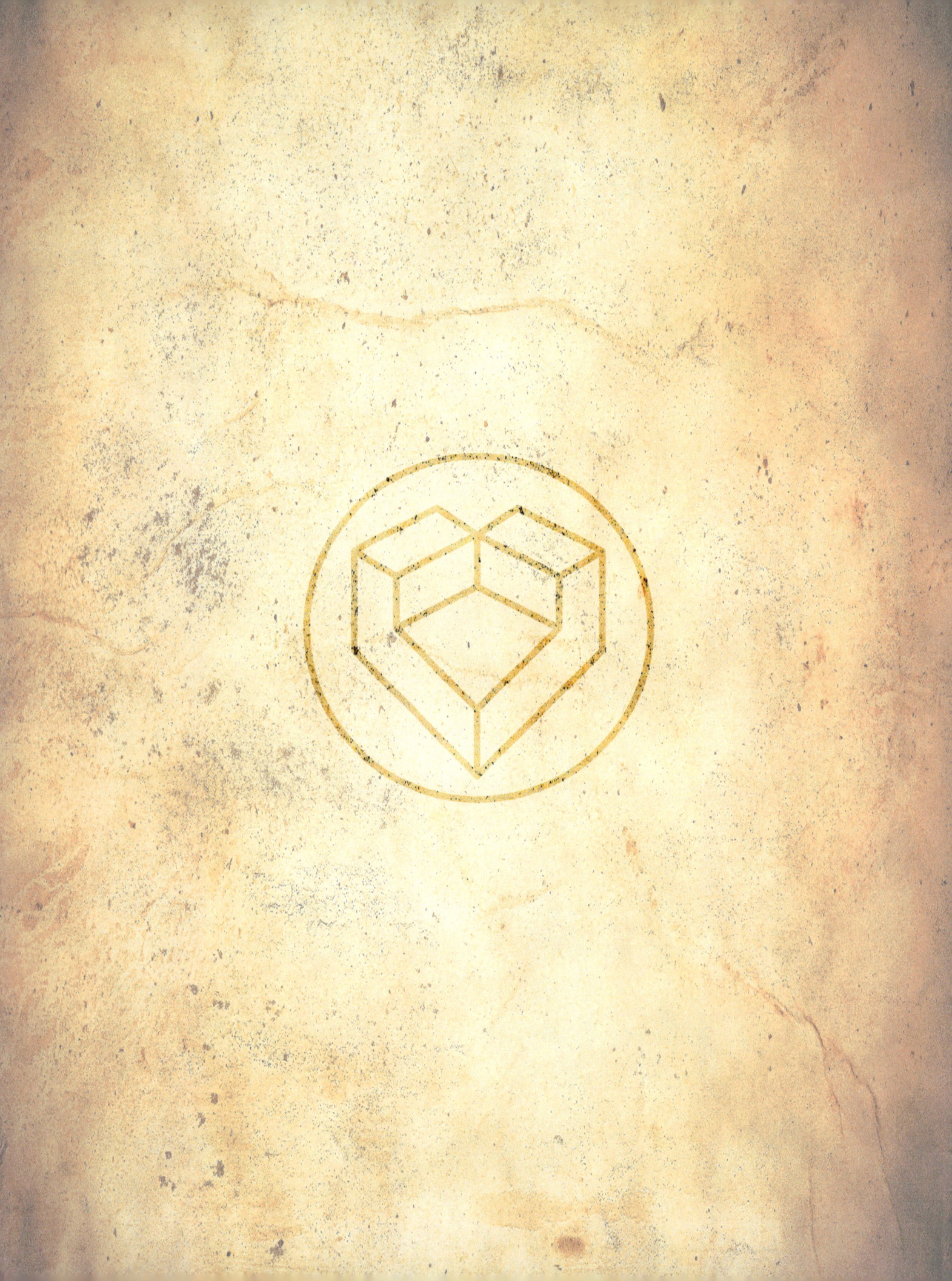

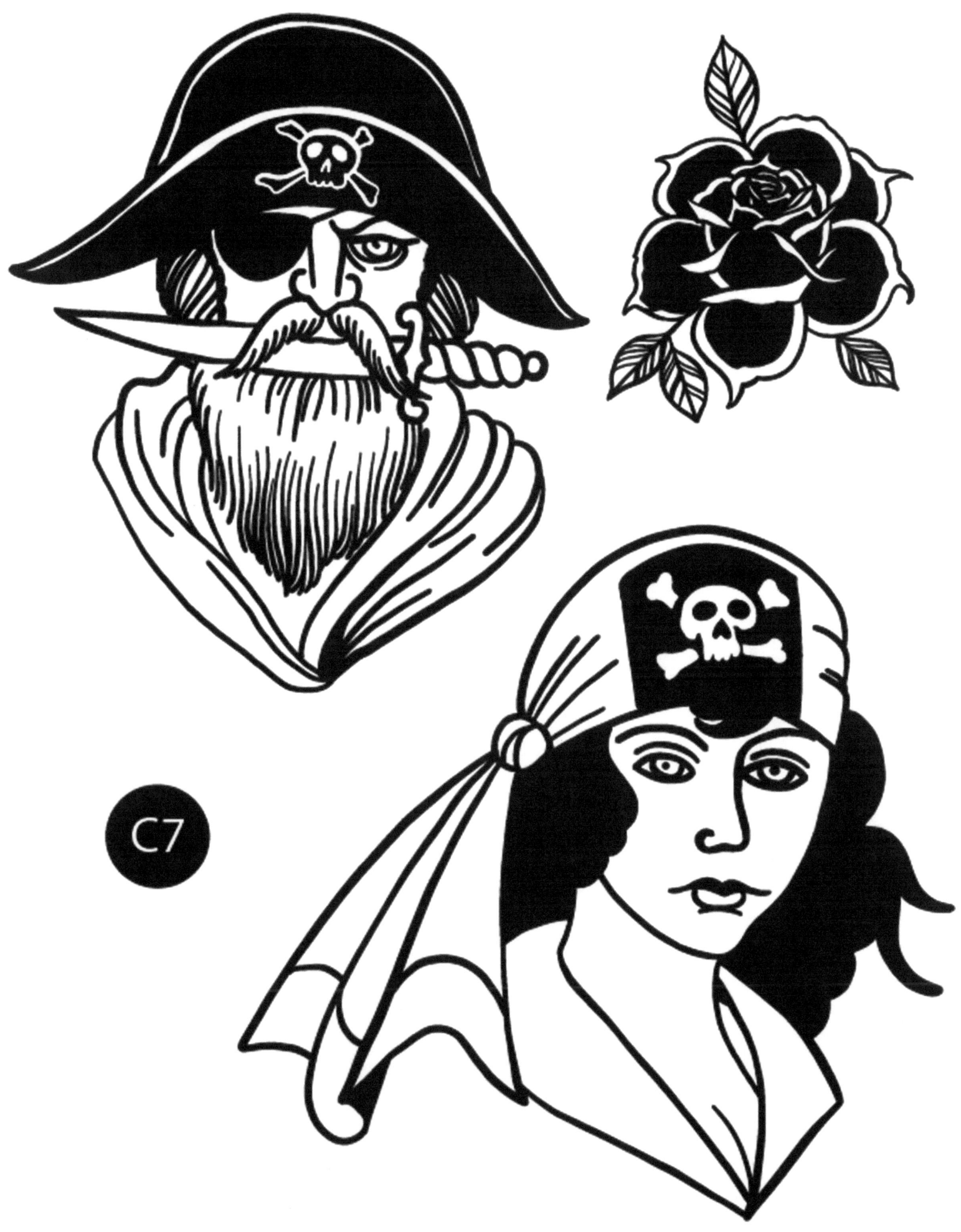

C7

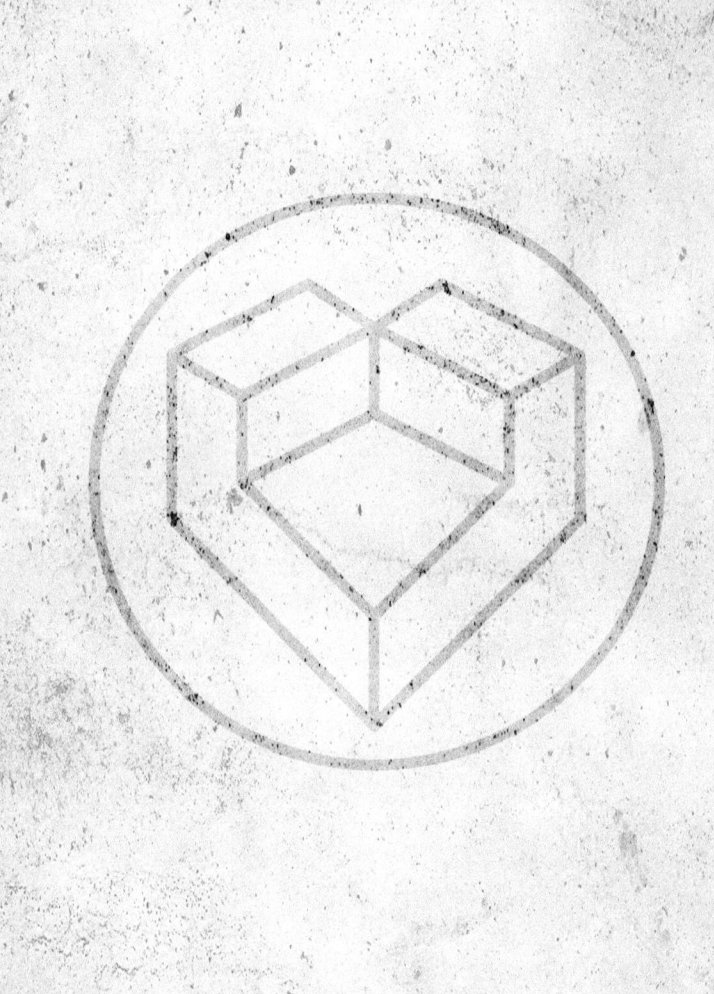

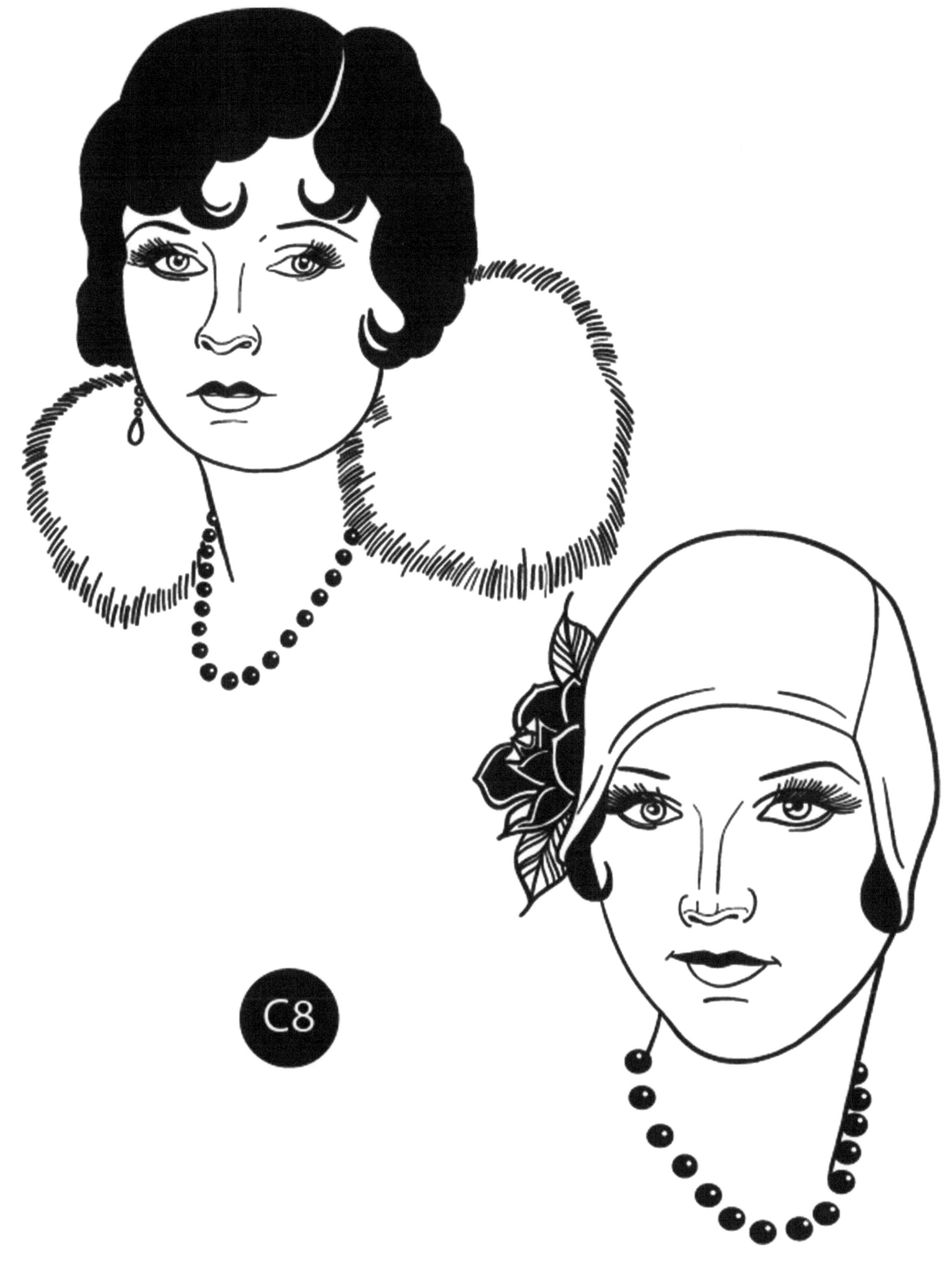

C8

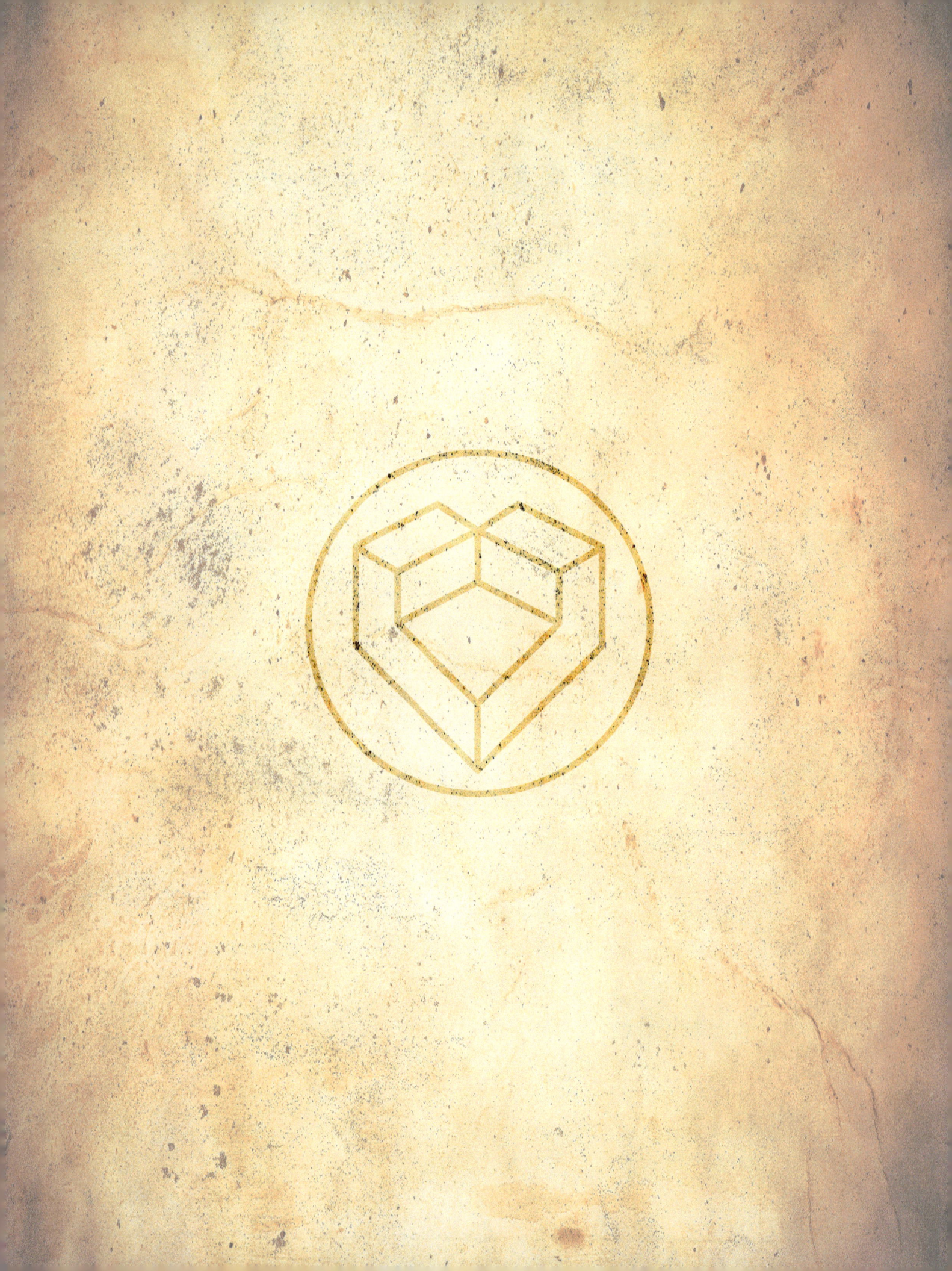

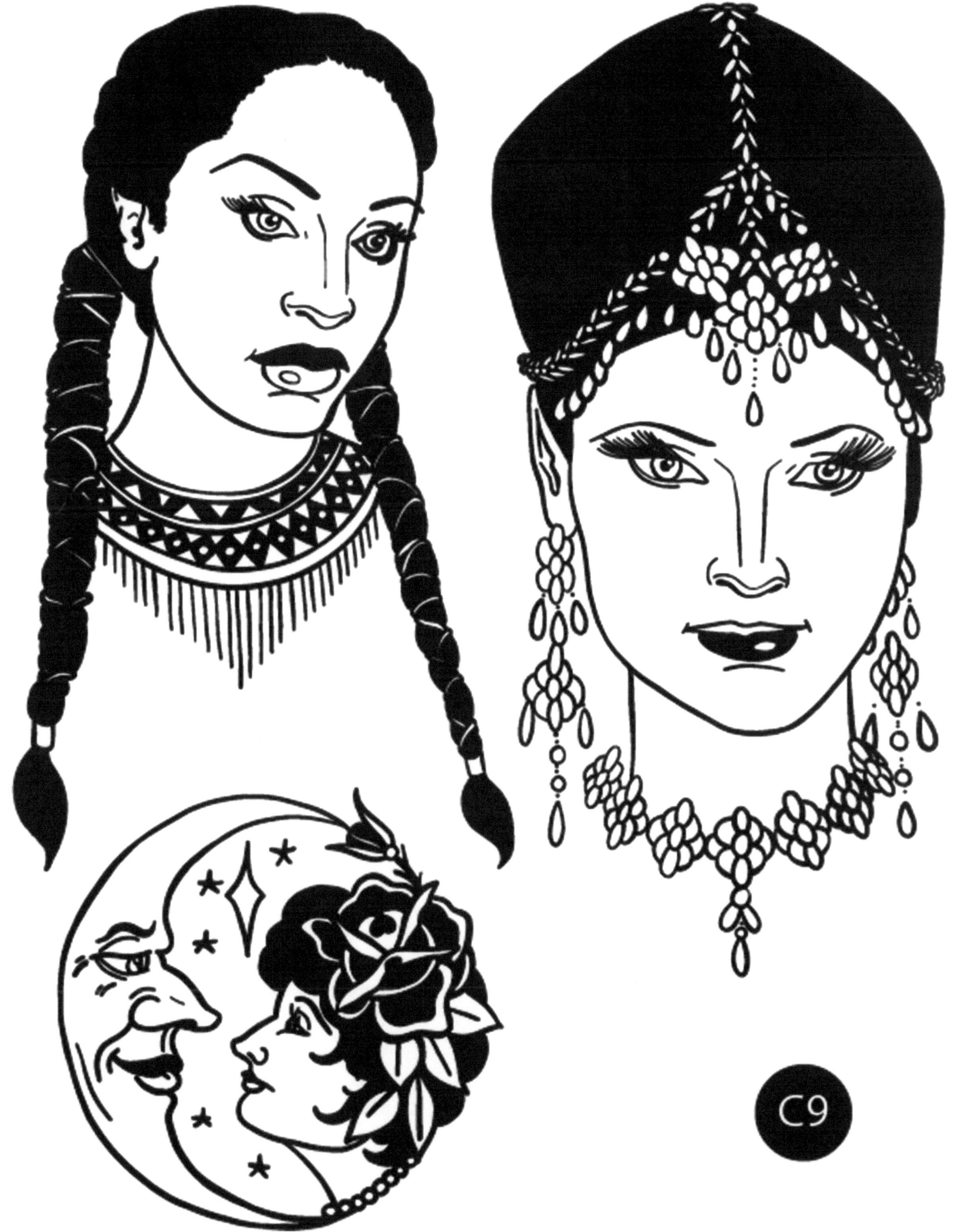

C9

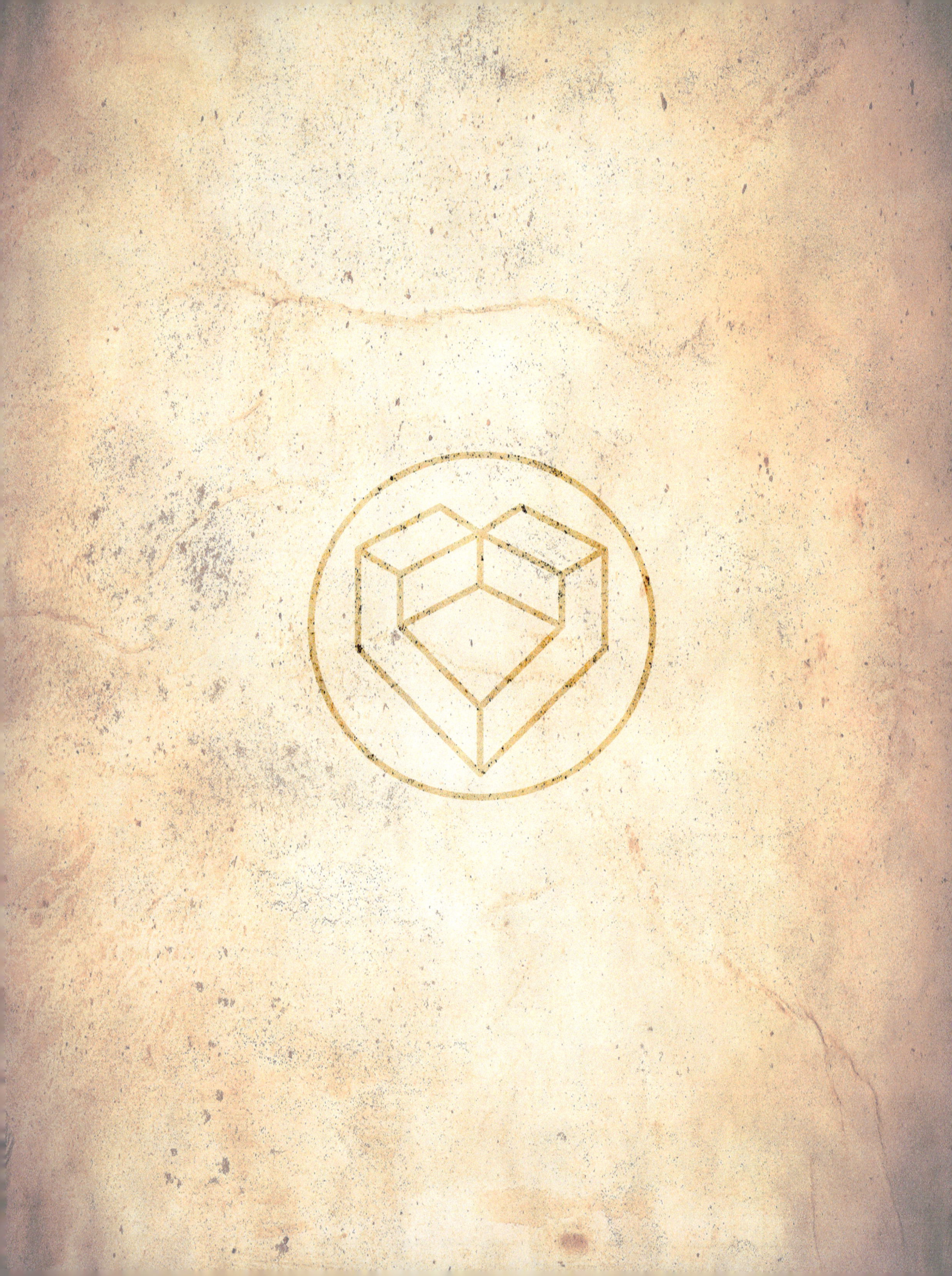

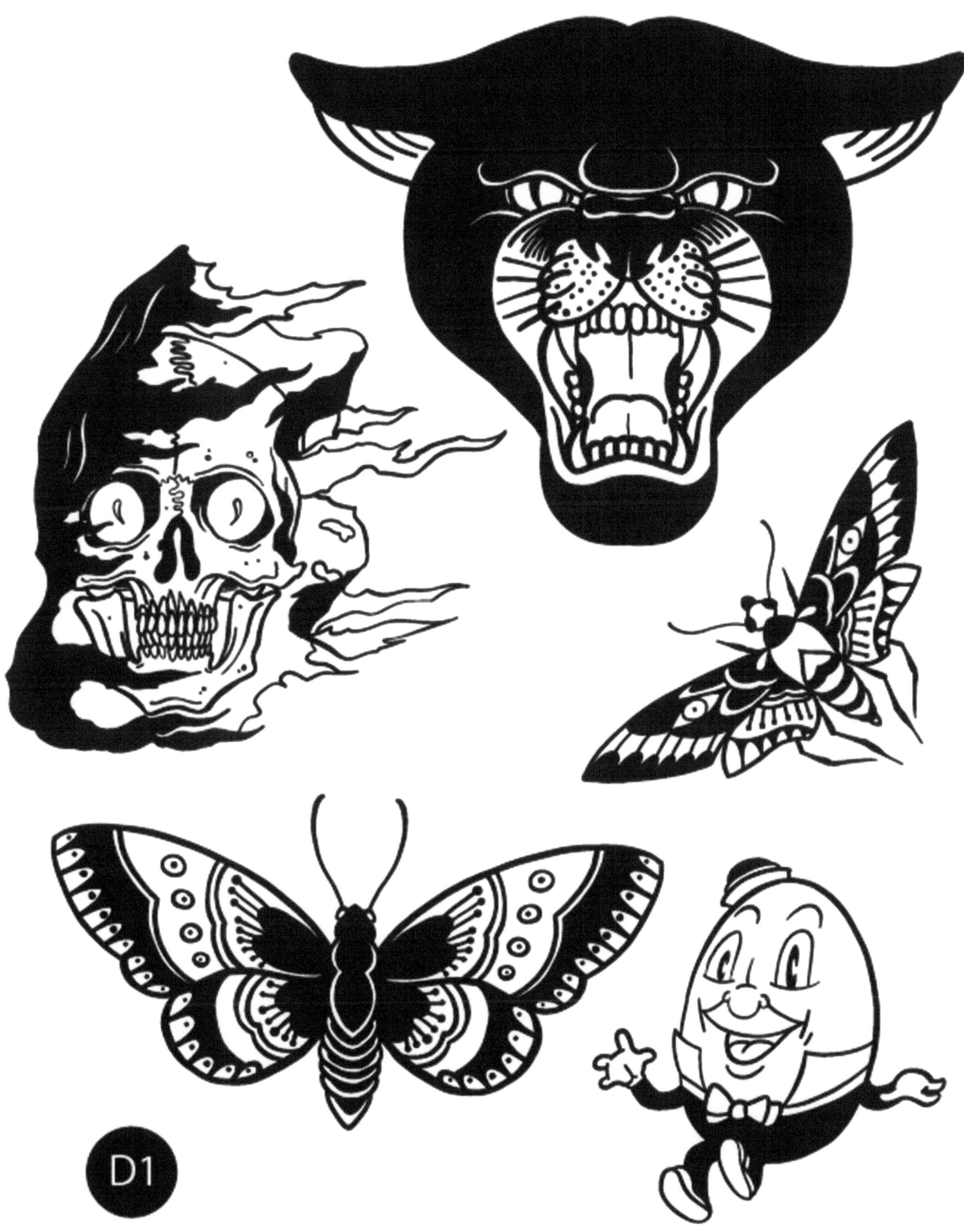

D1

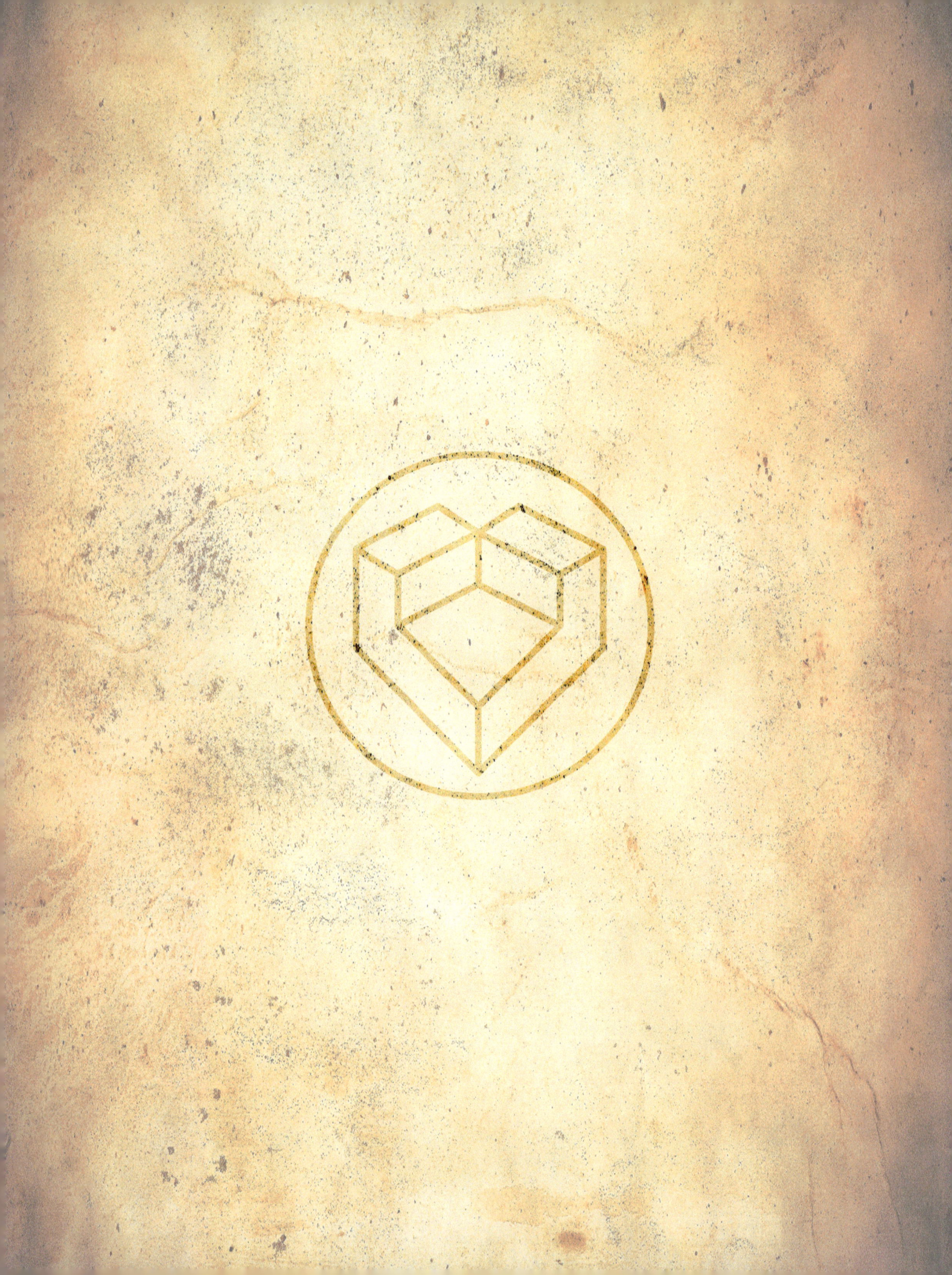

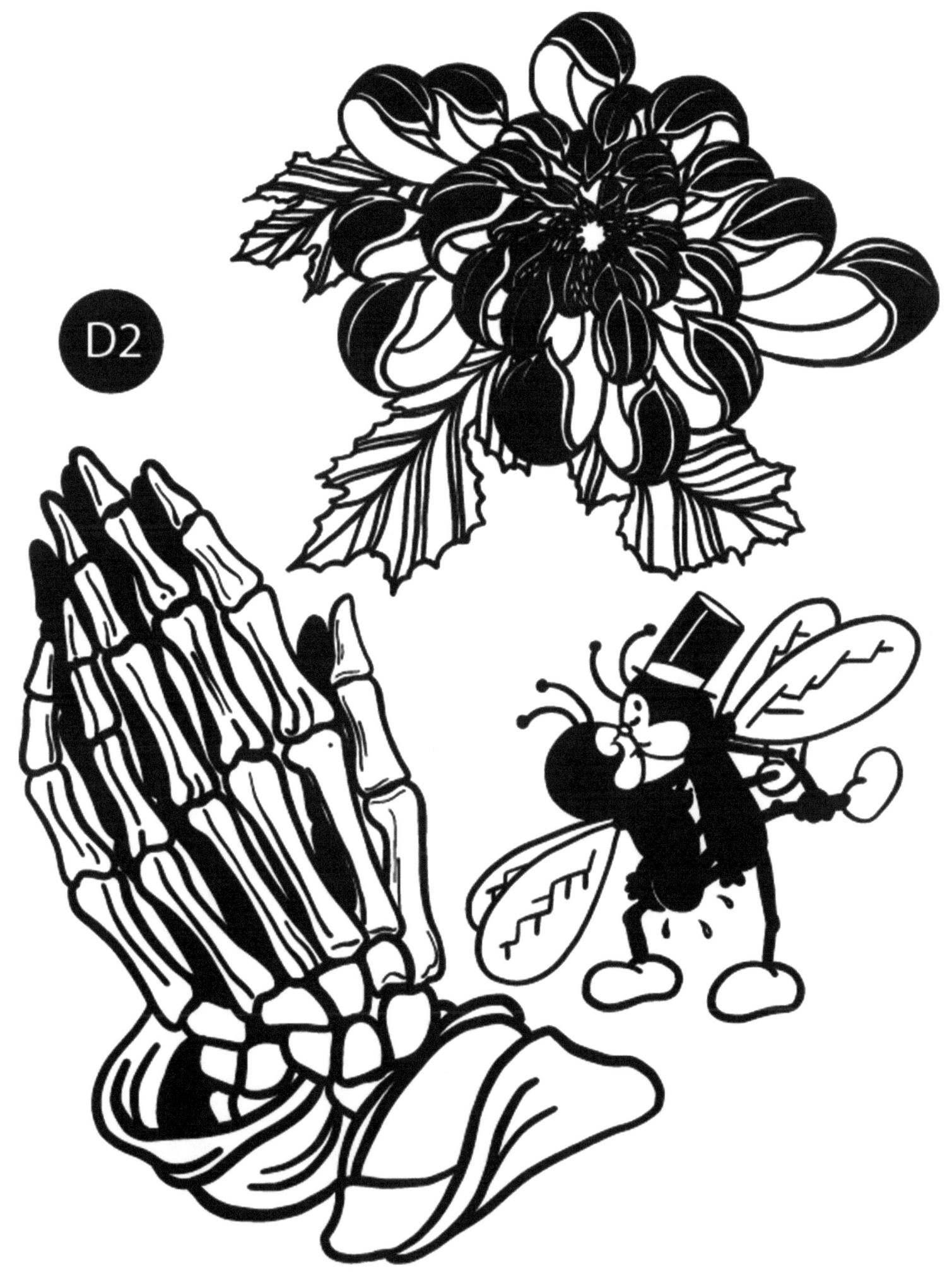

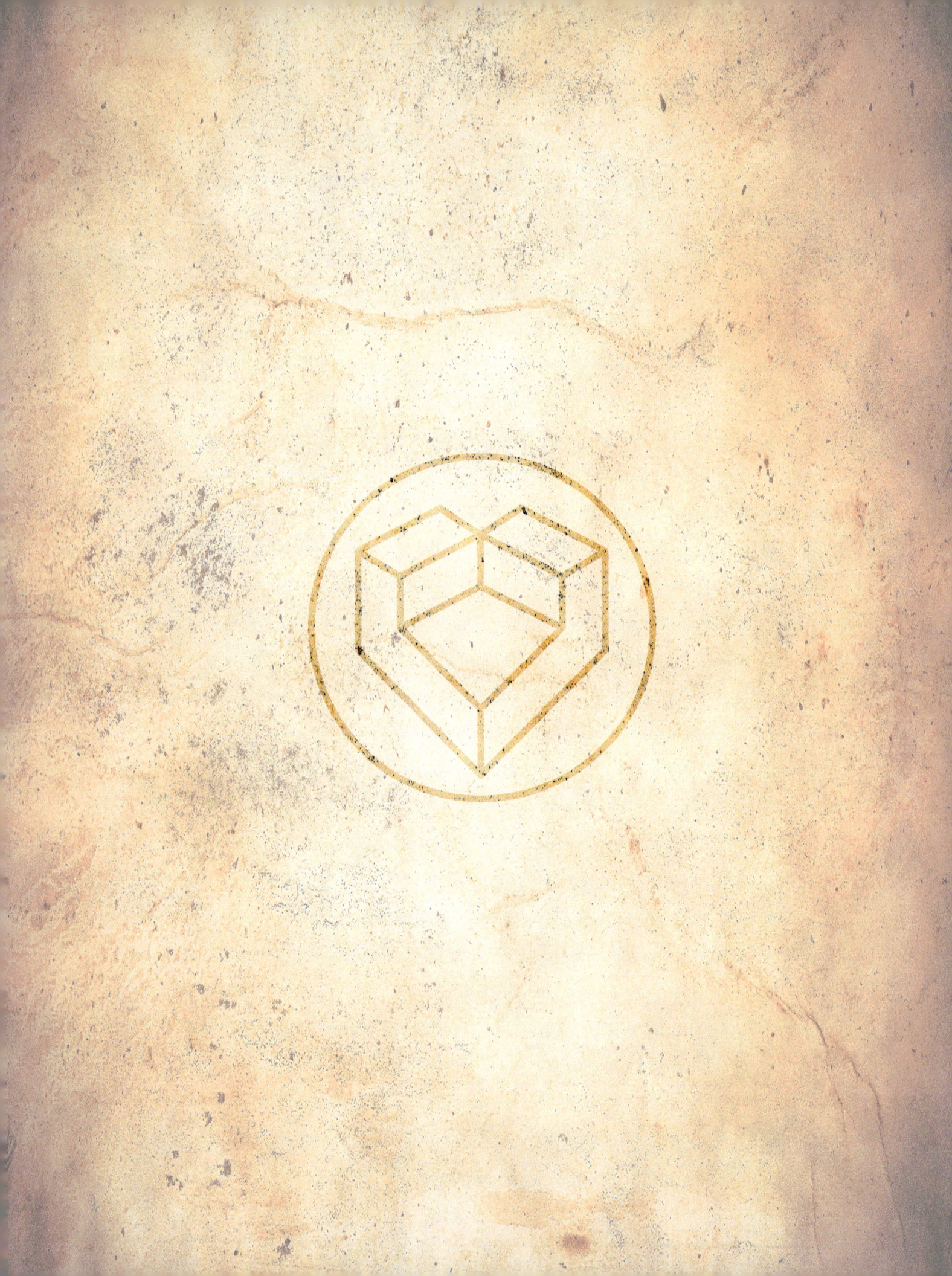

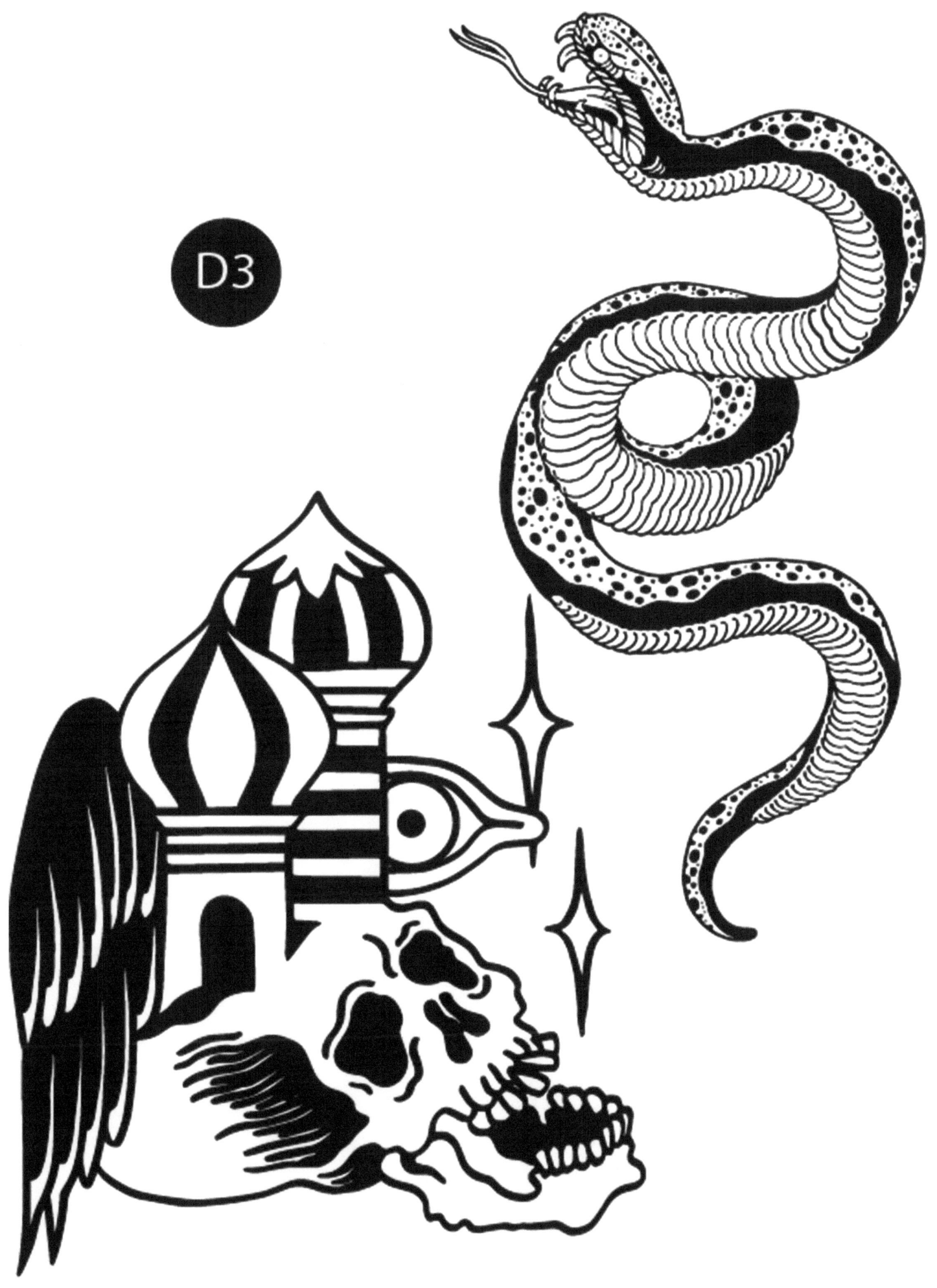

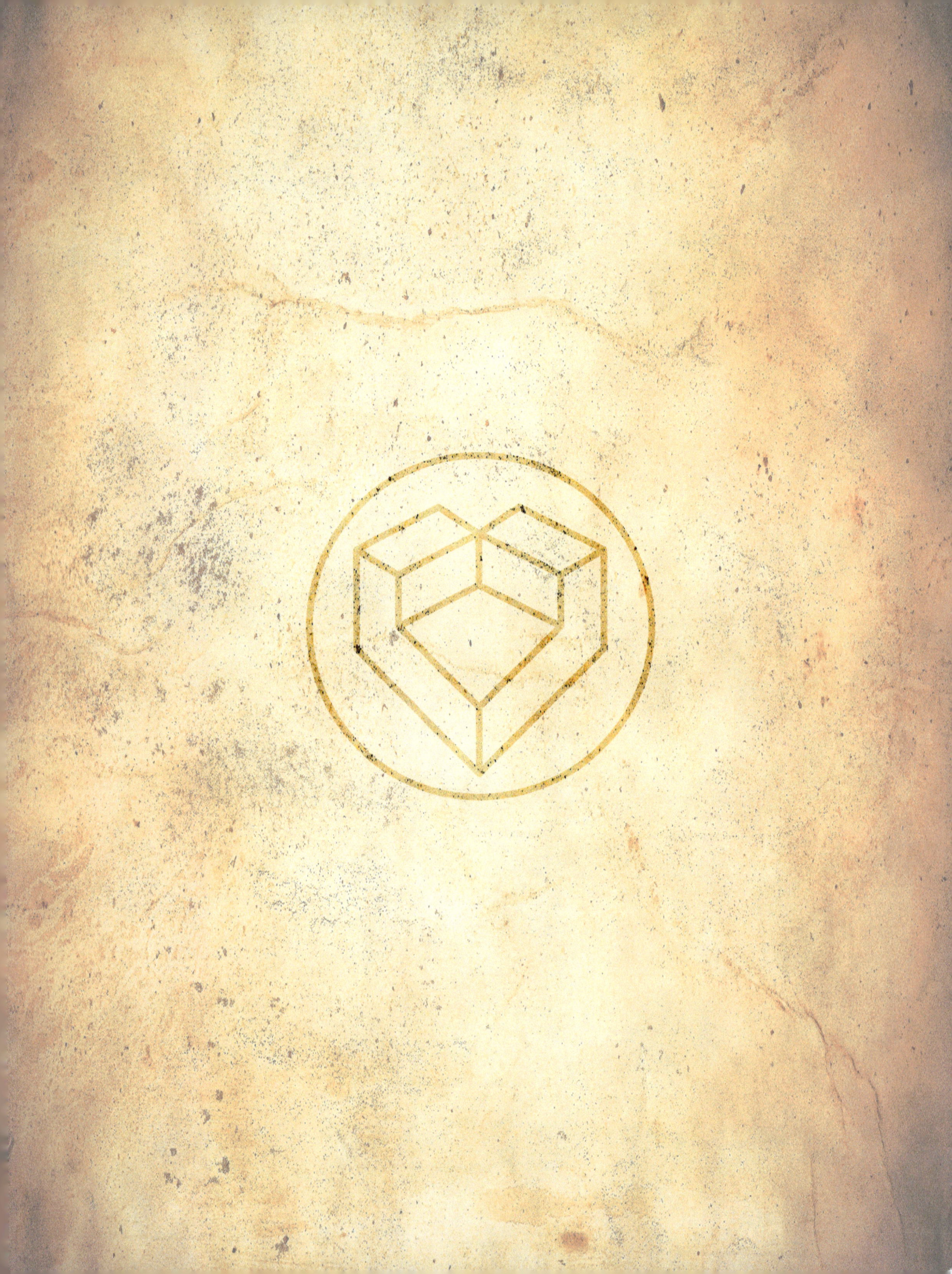

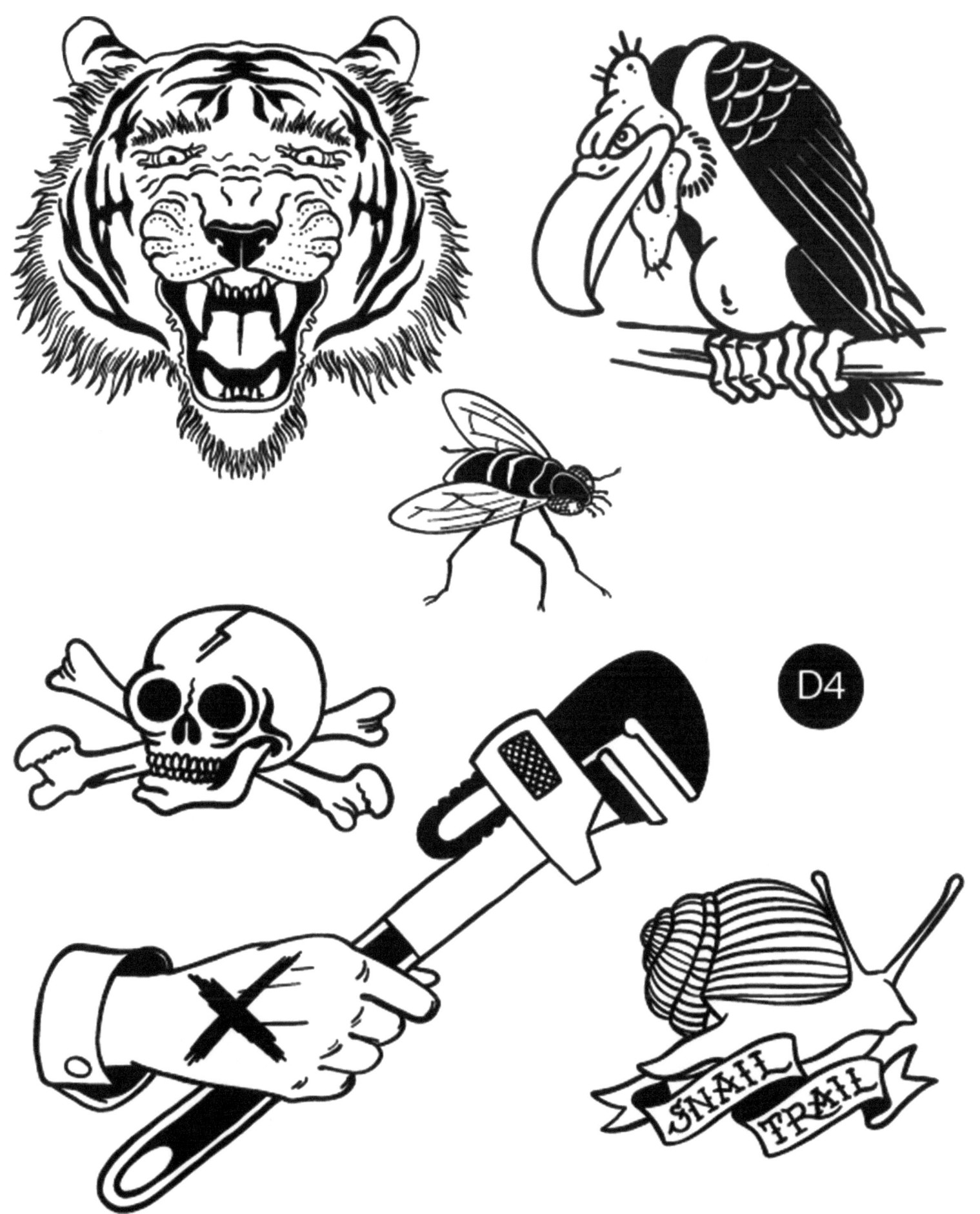

D4

SNAIL TRAIL

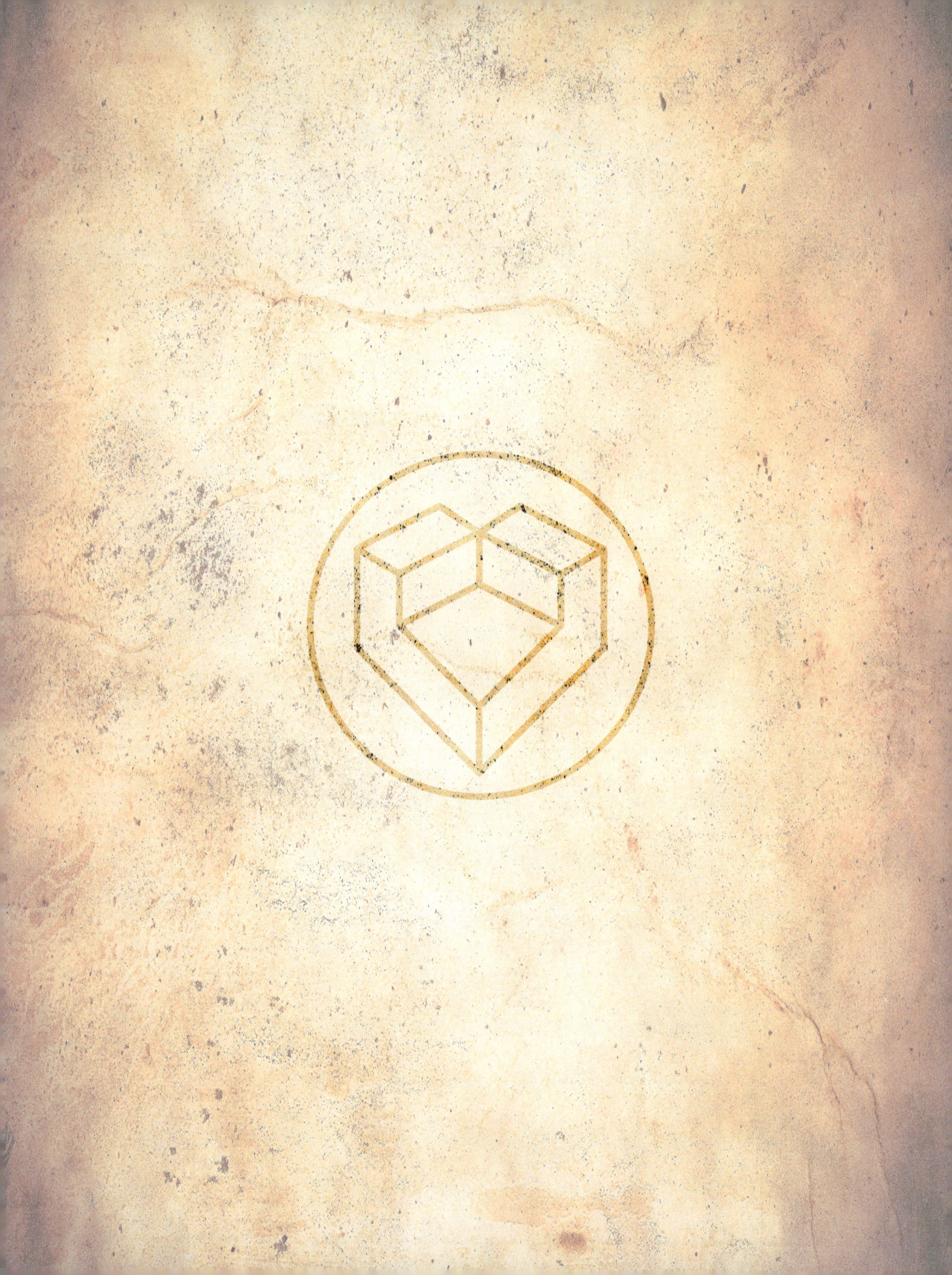

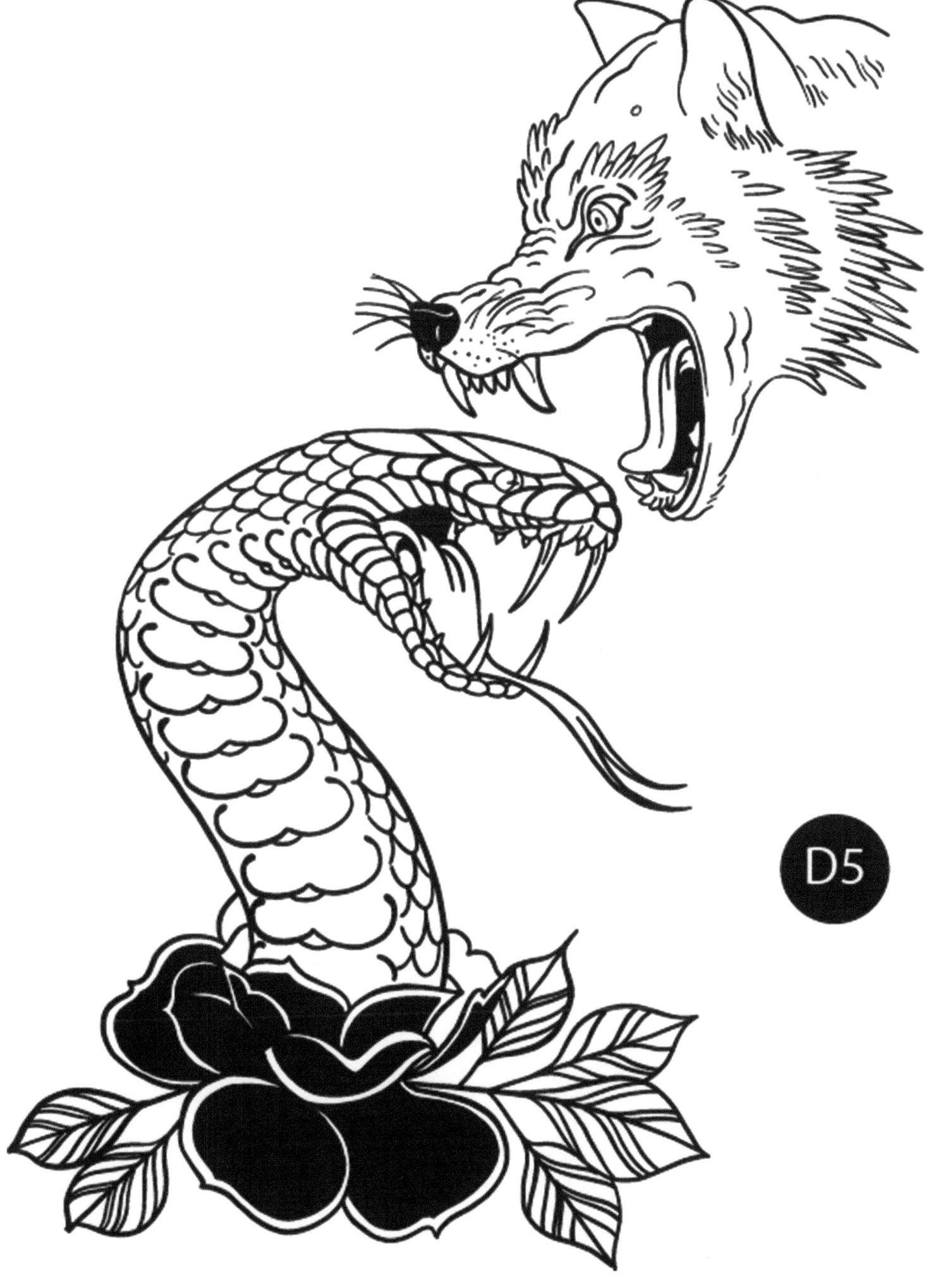

D5

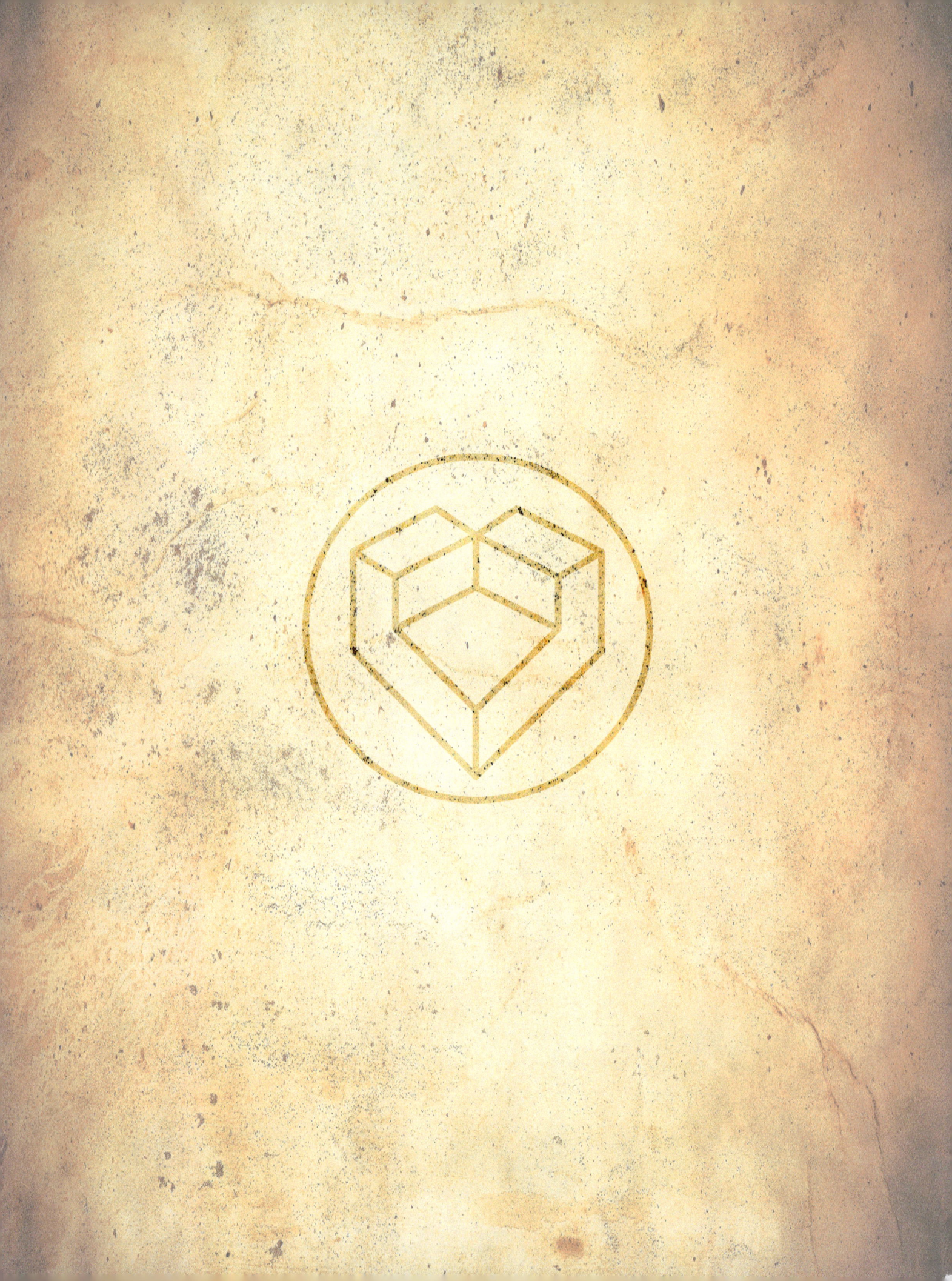

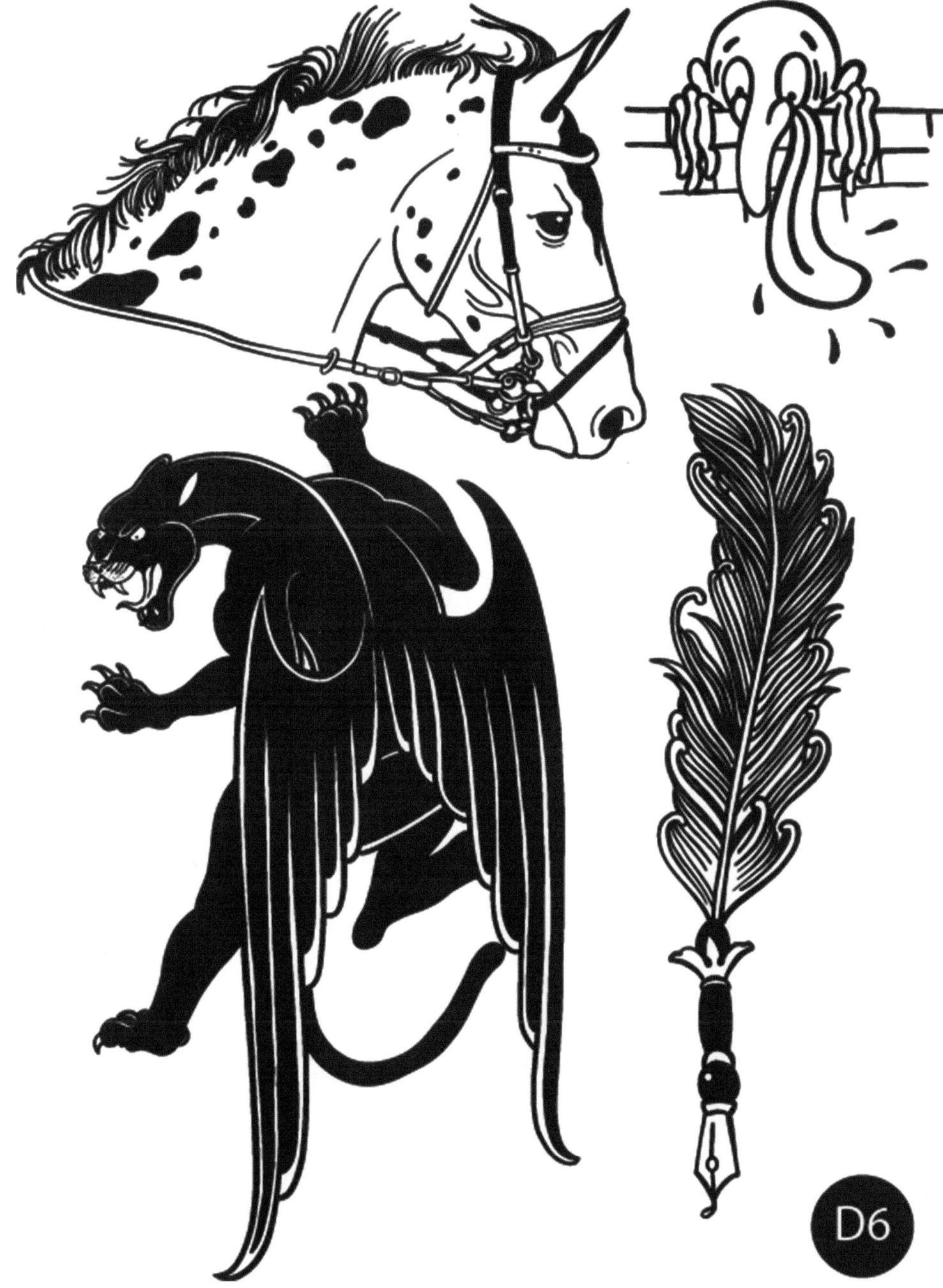

D6

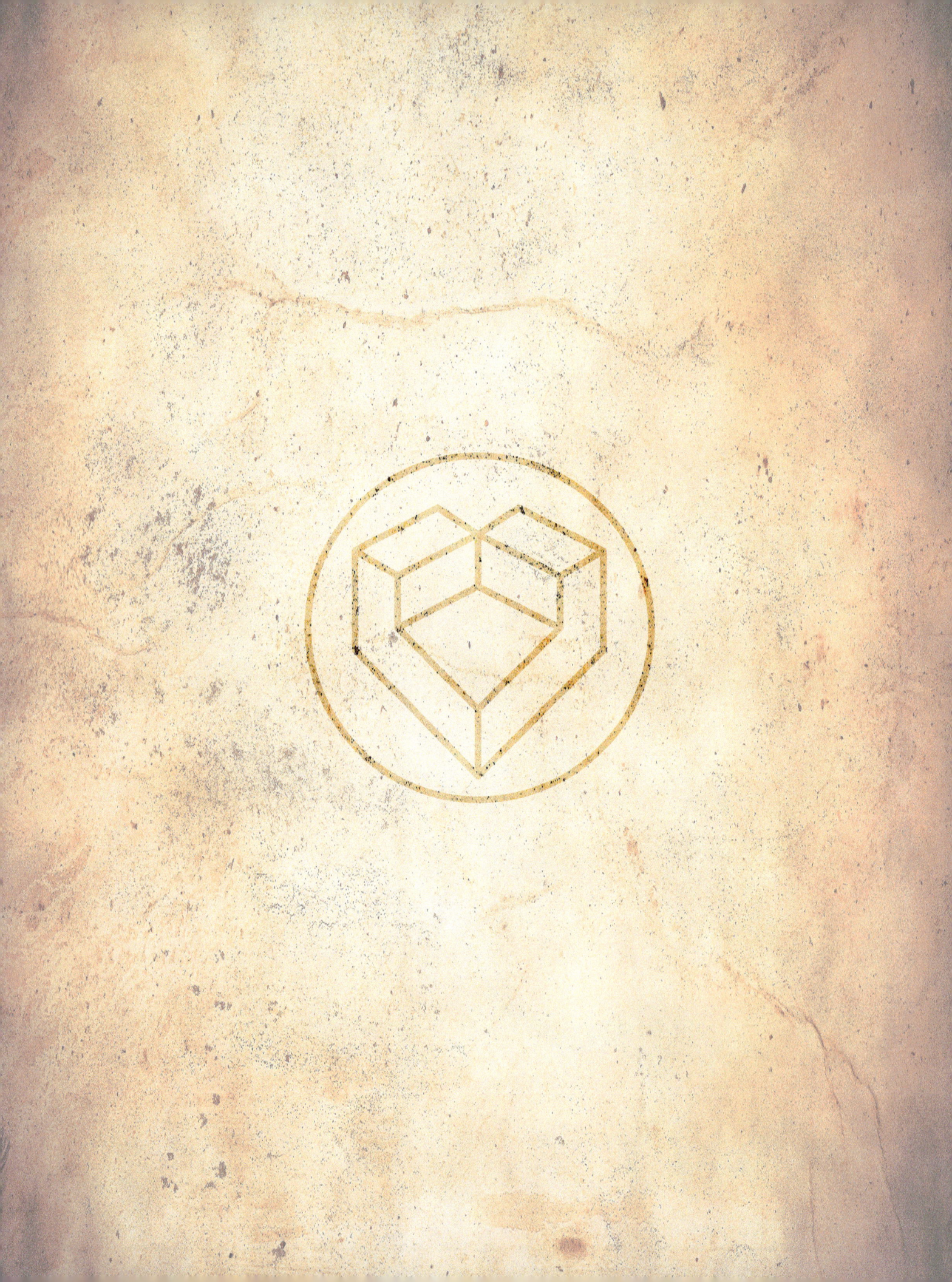

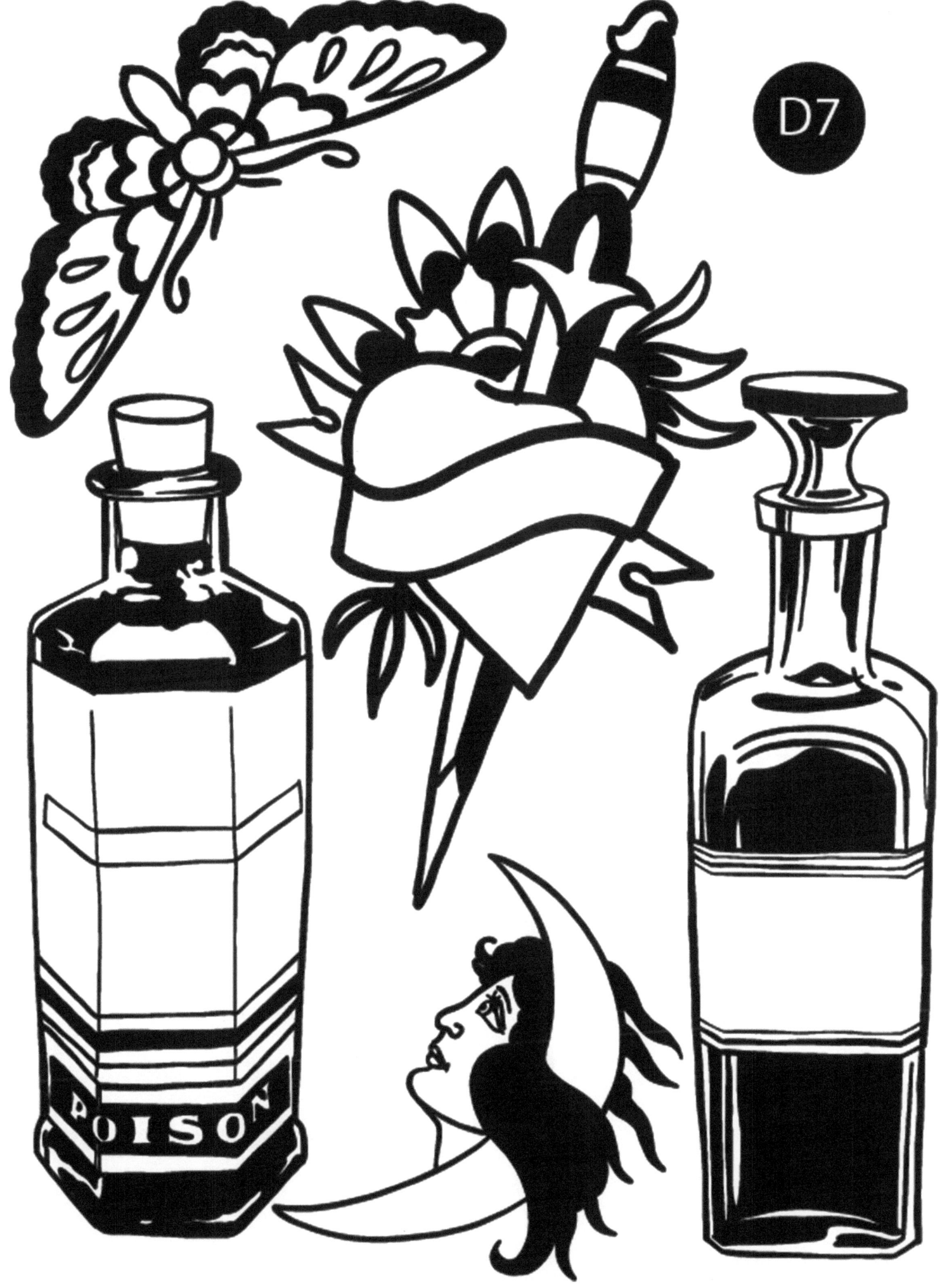

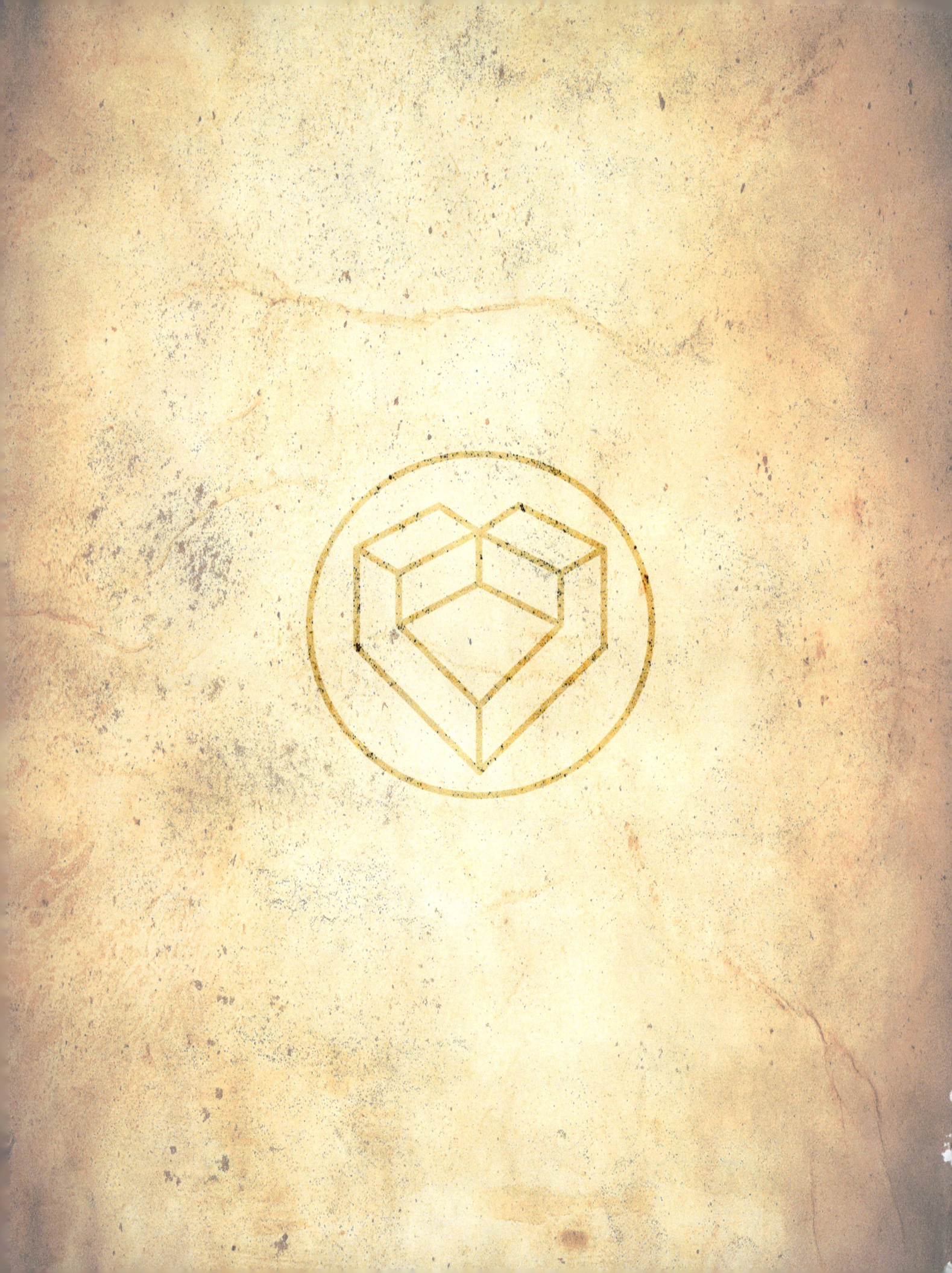

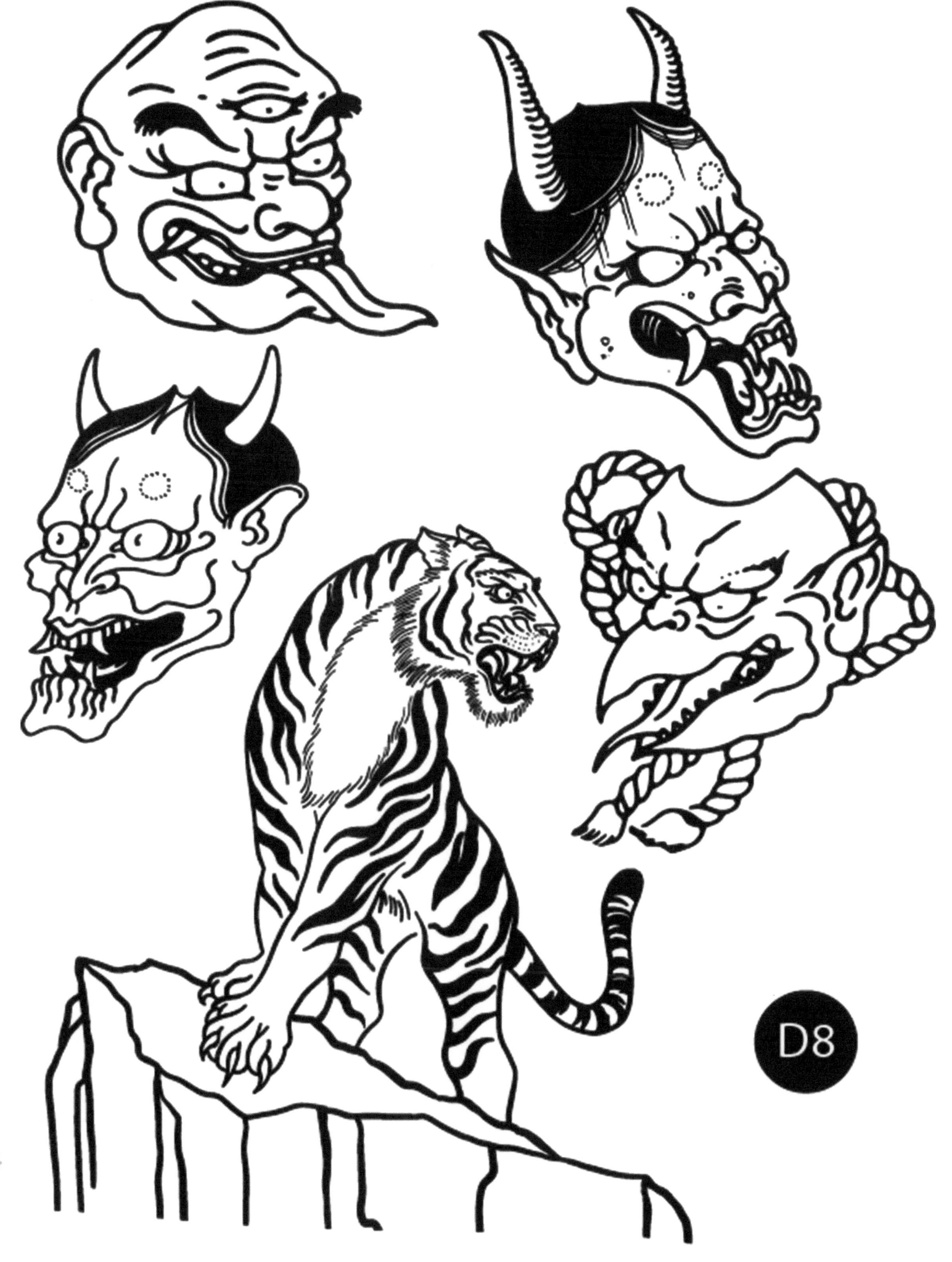

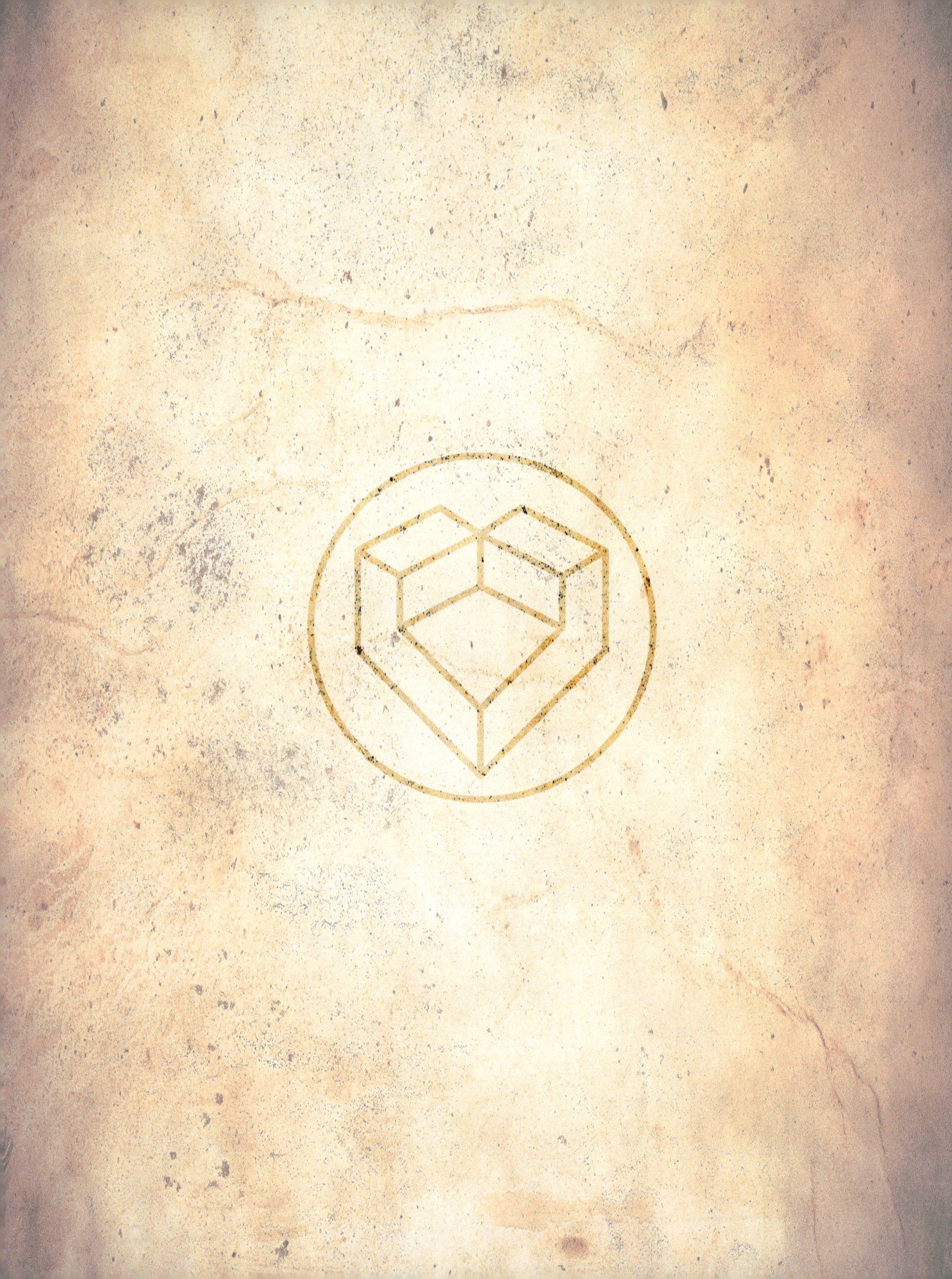

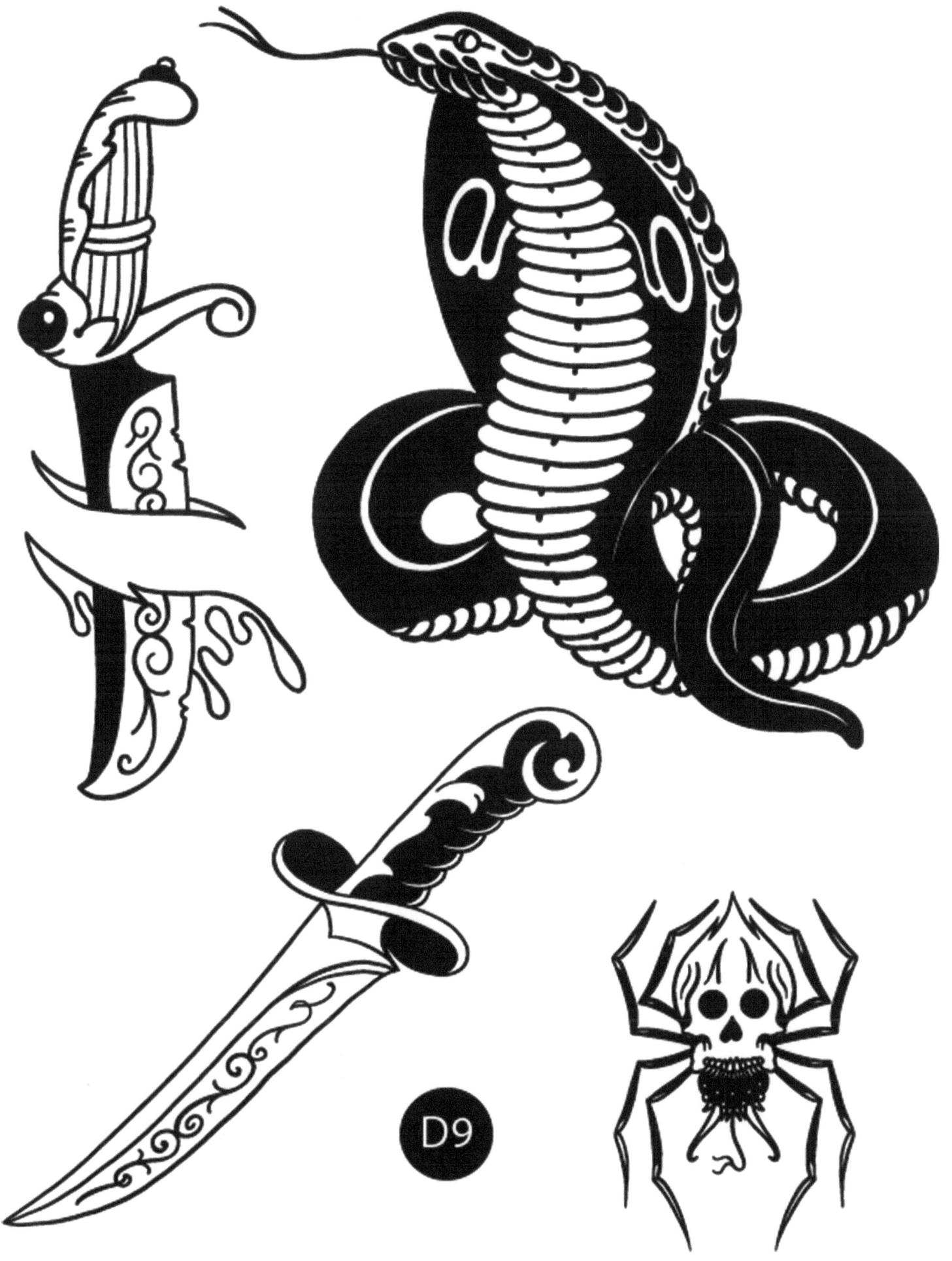

D9

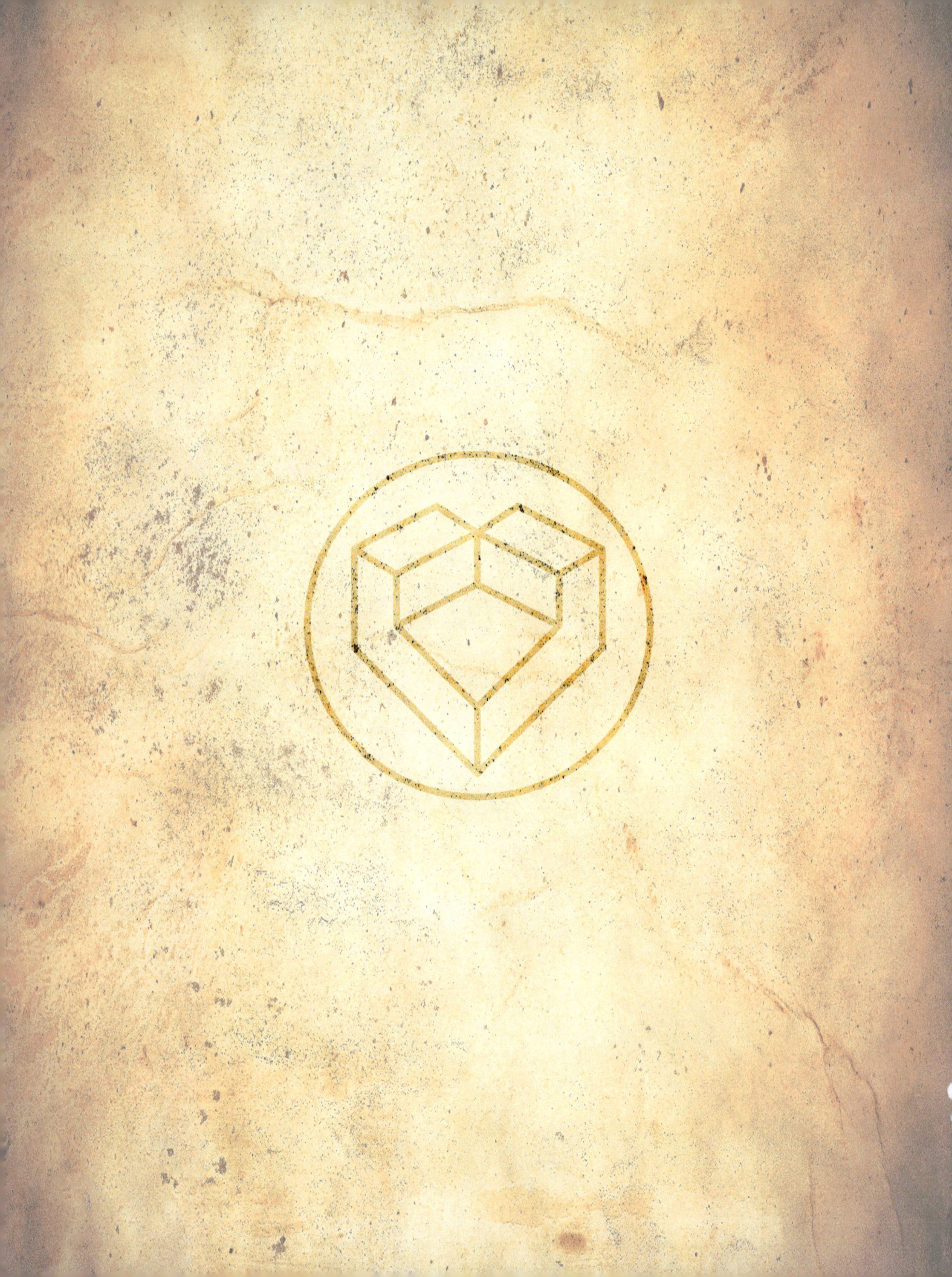

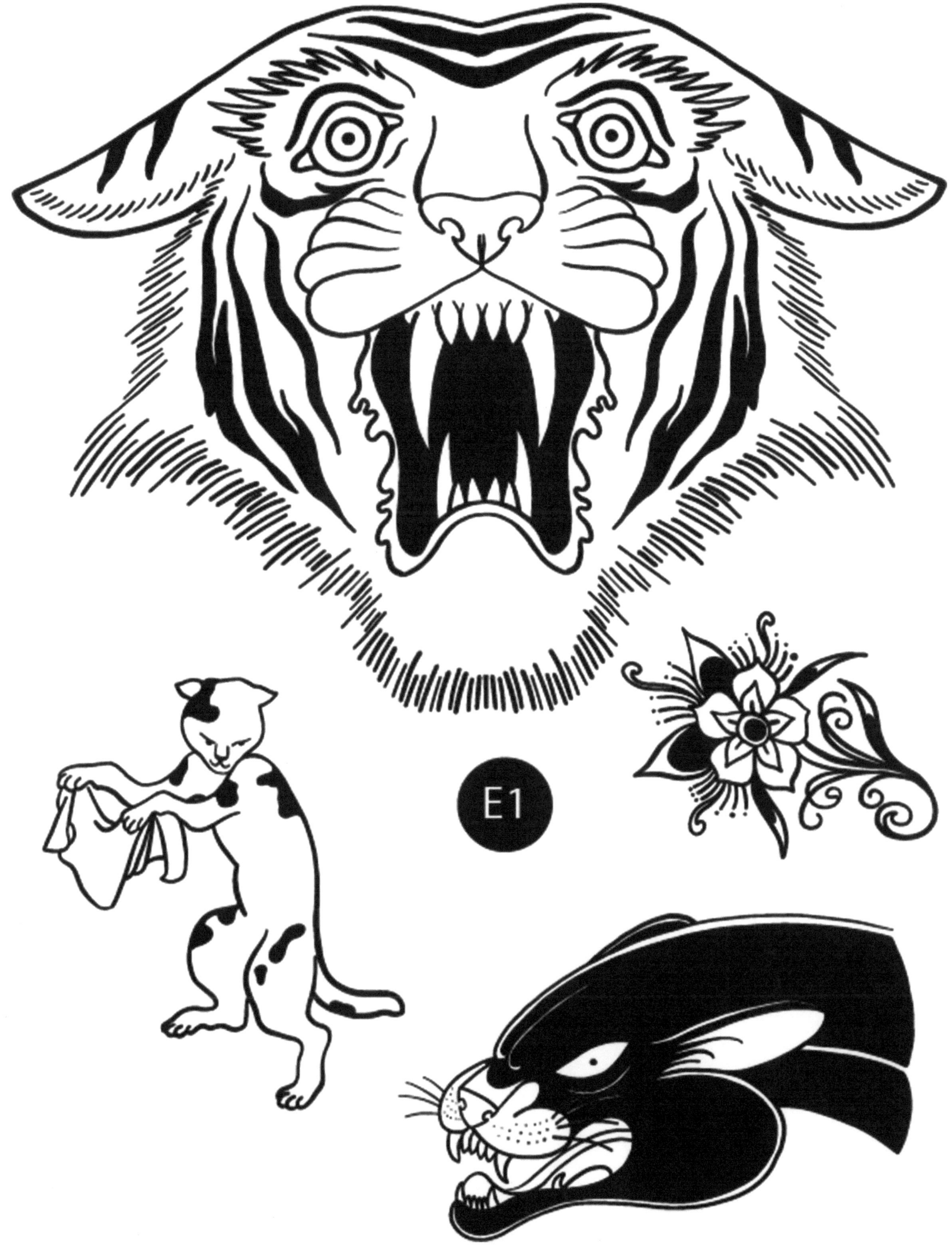

E1

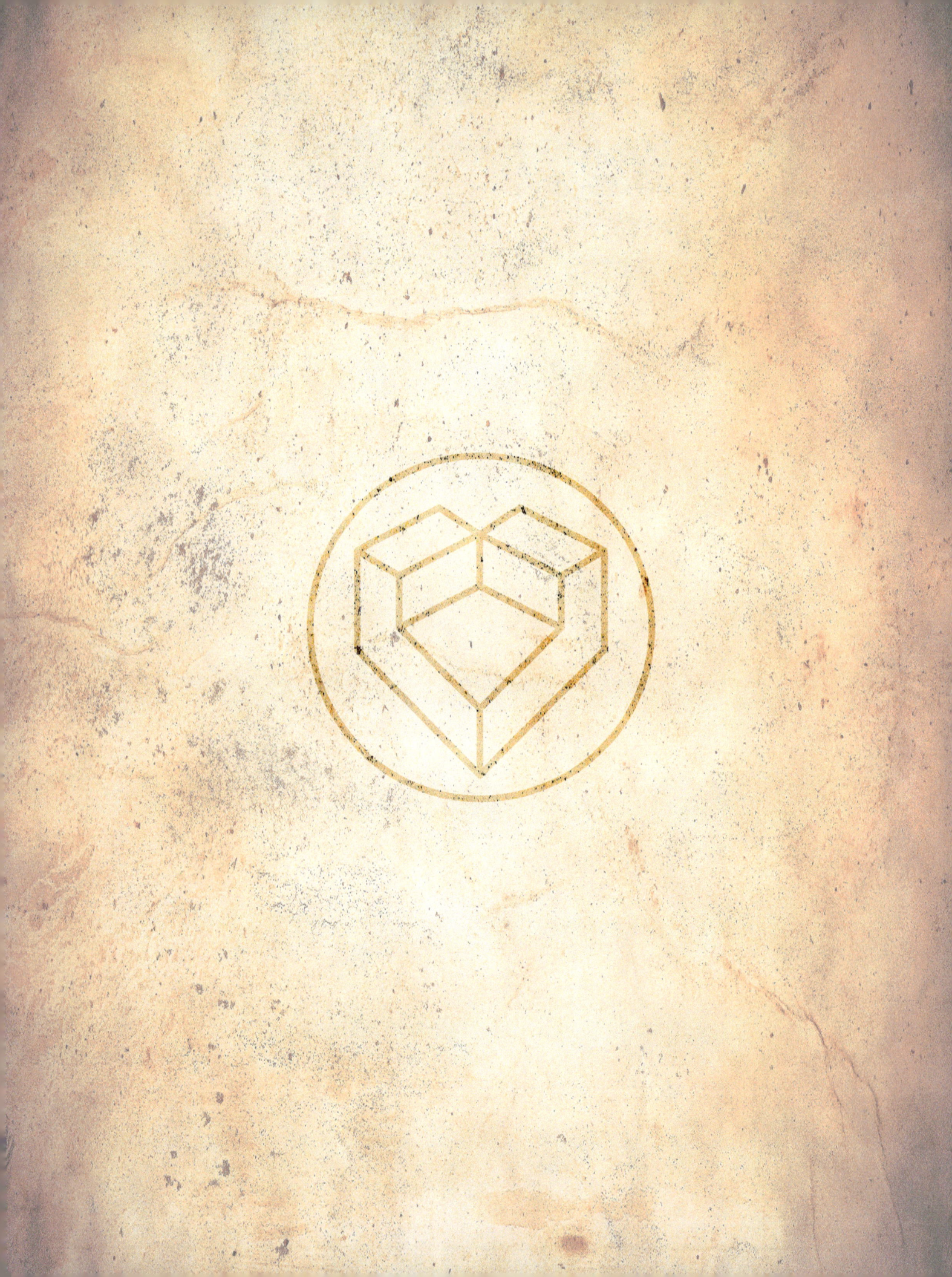

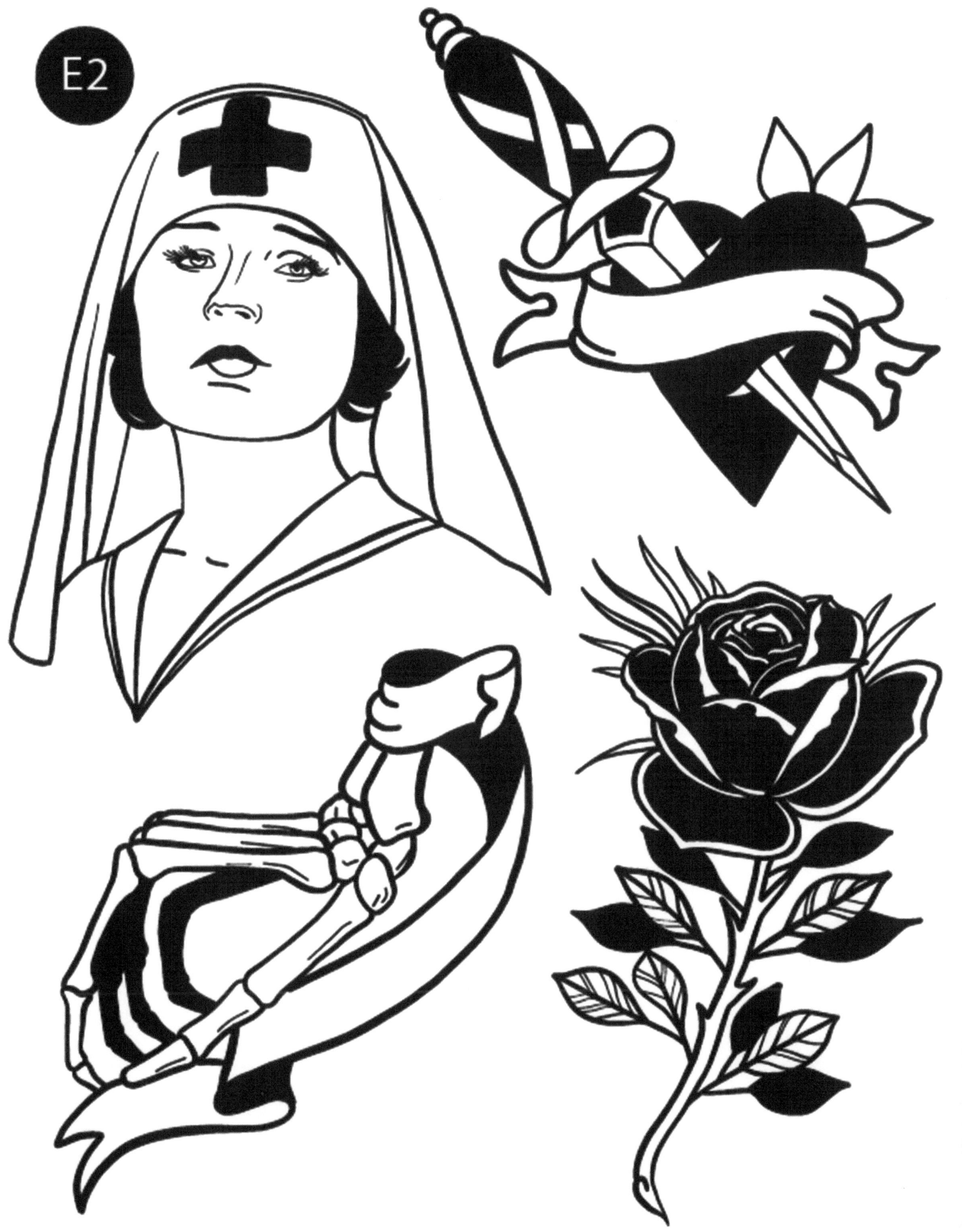

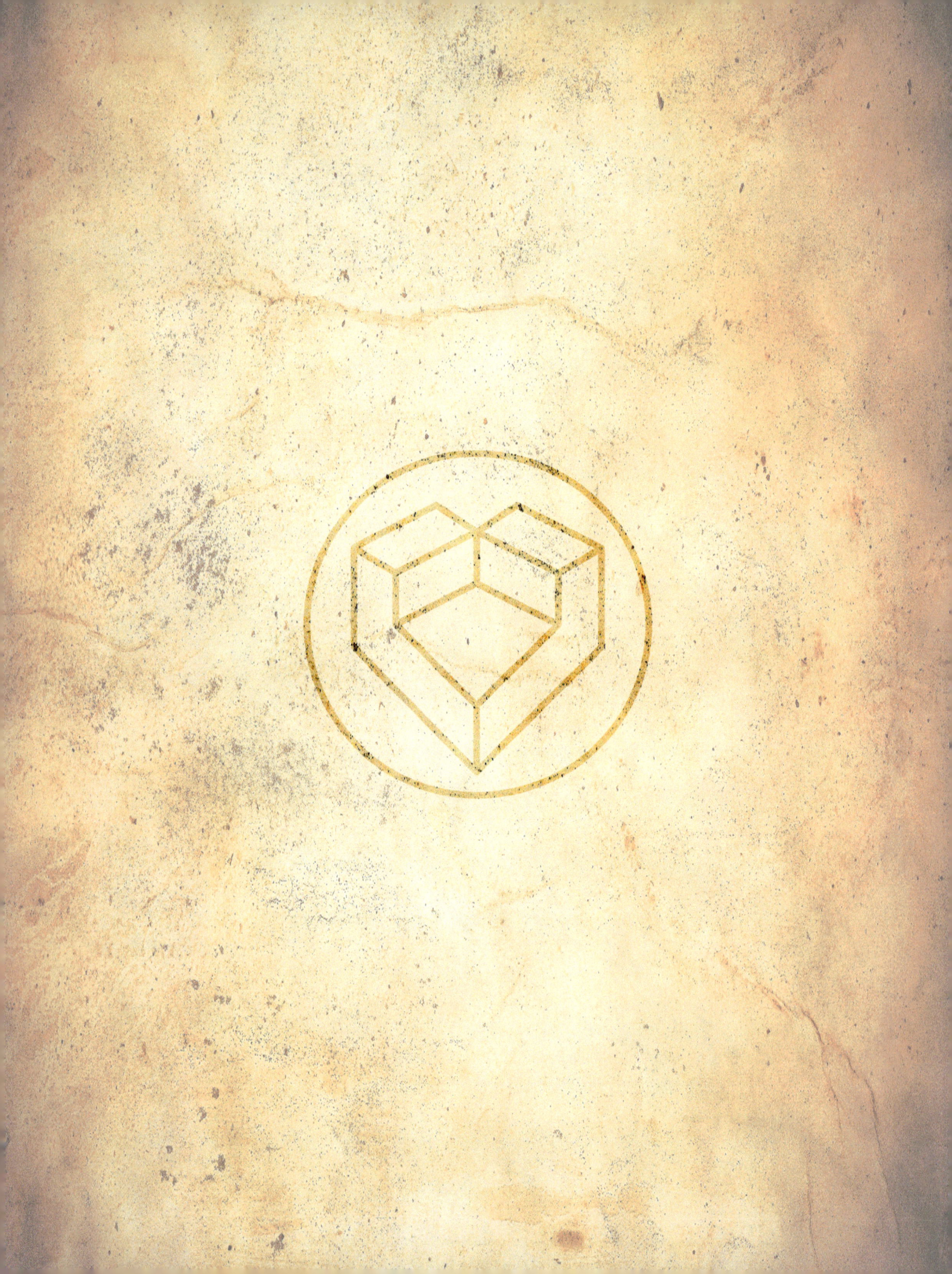

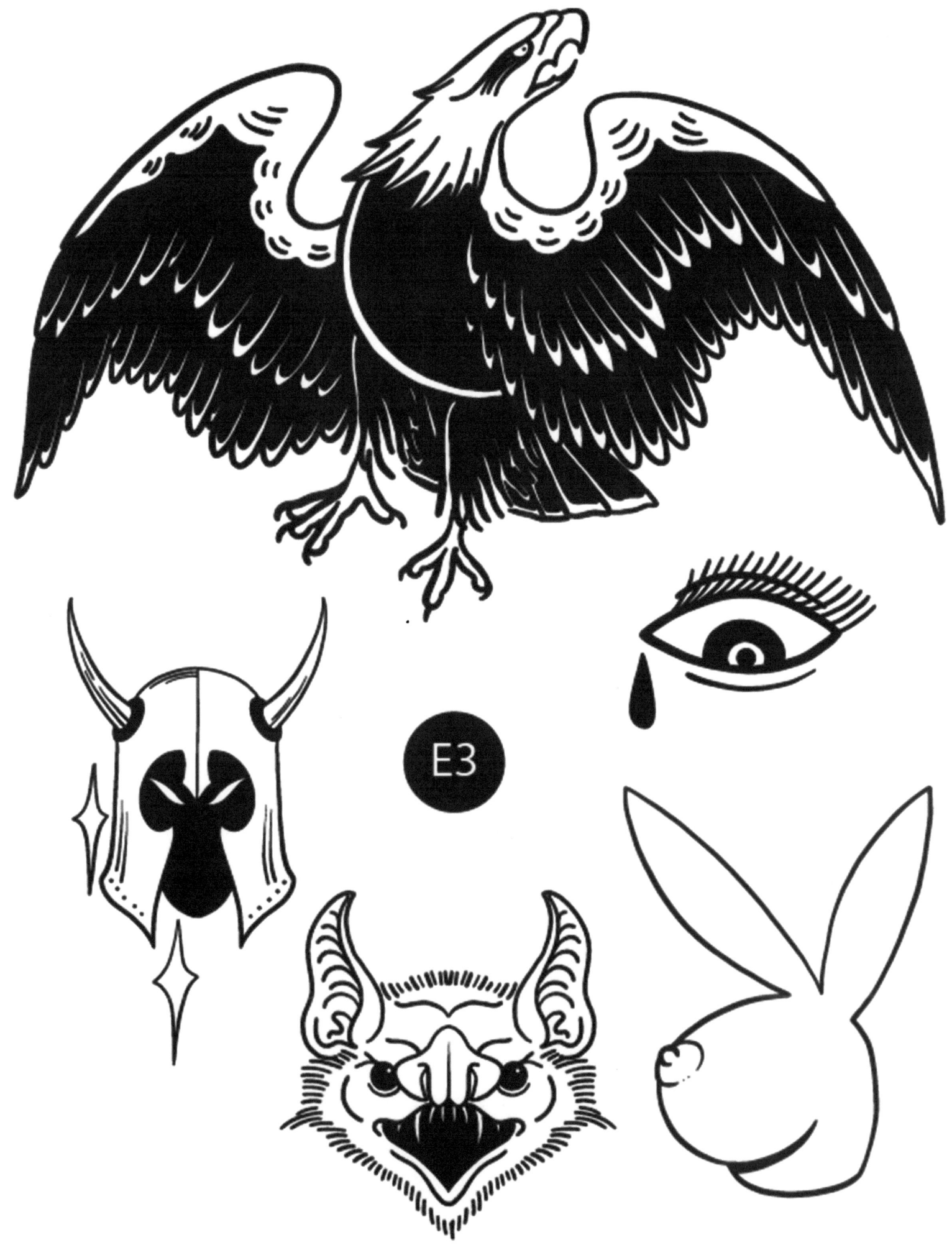

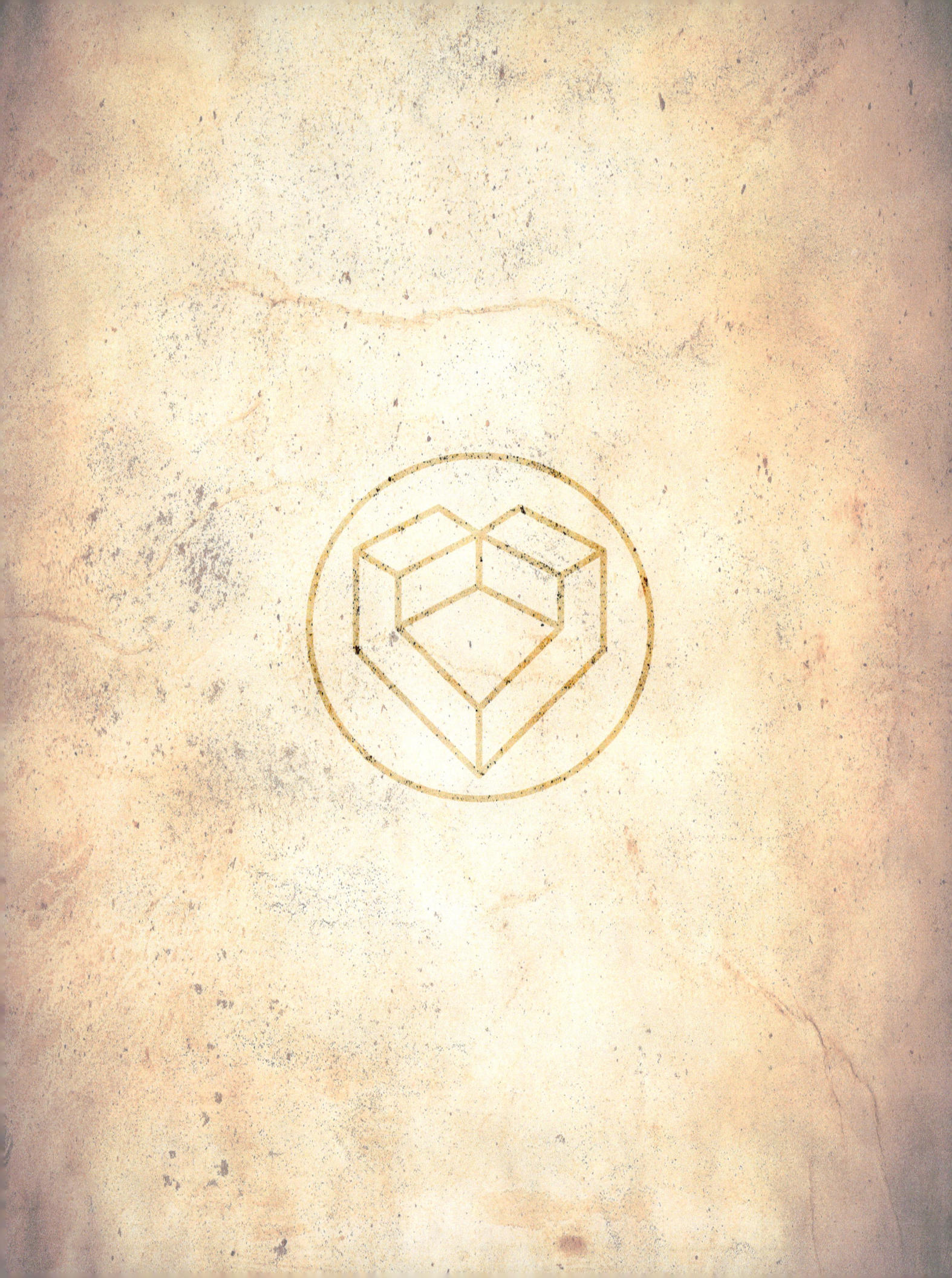

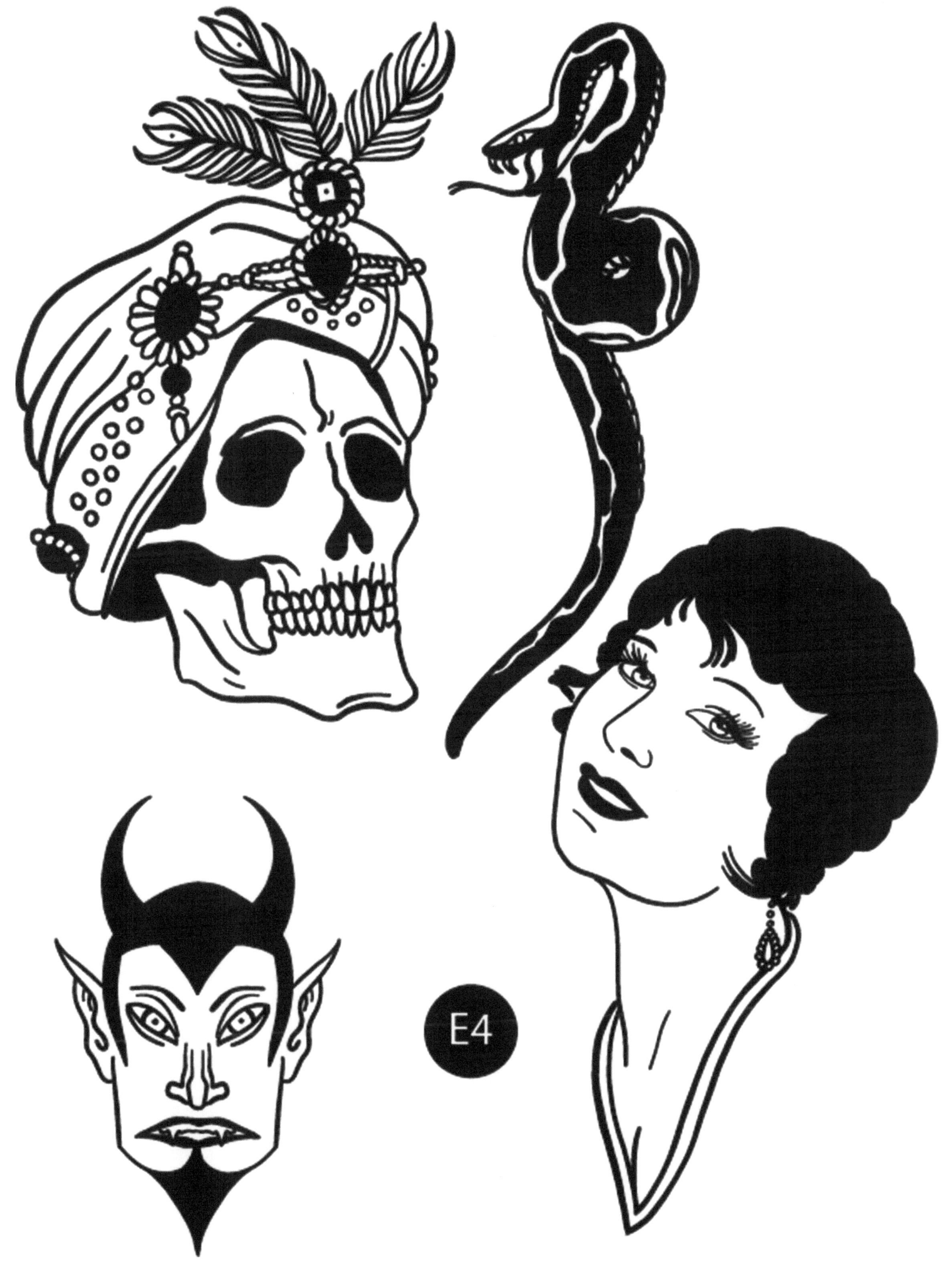

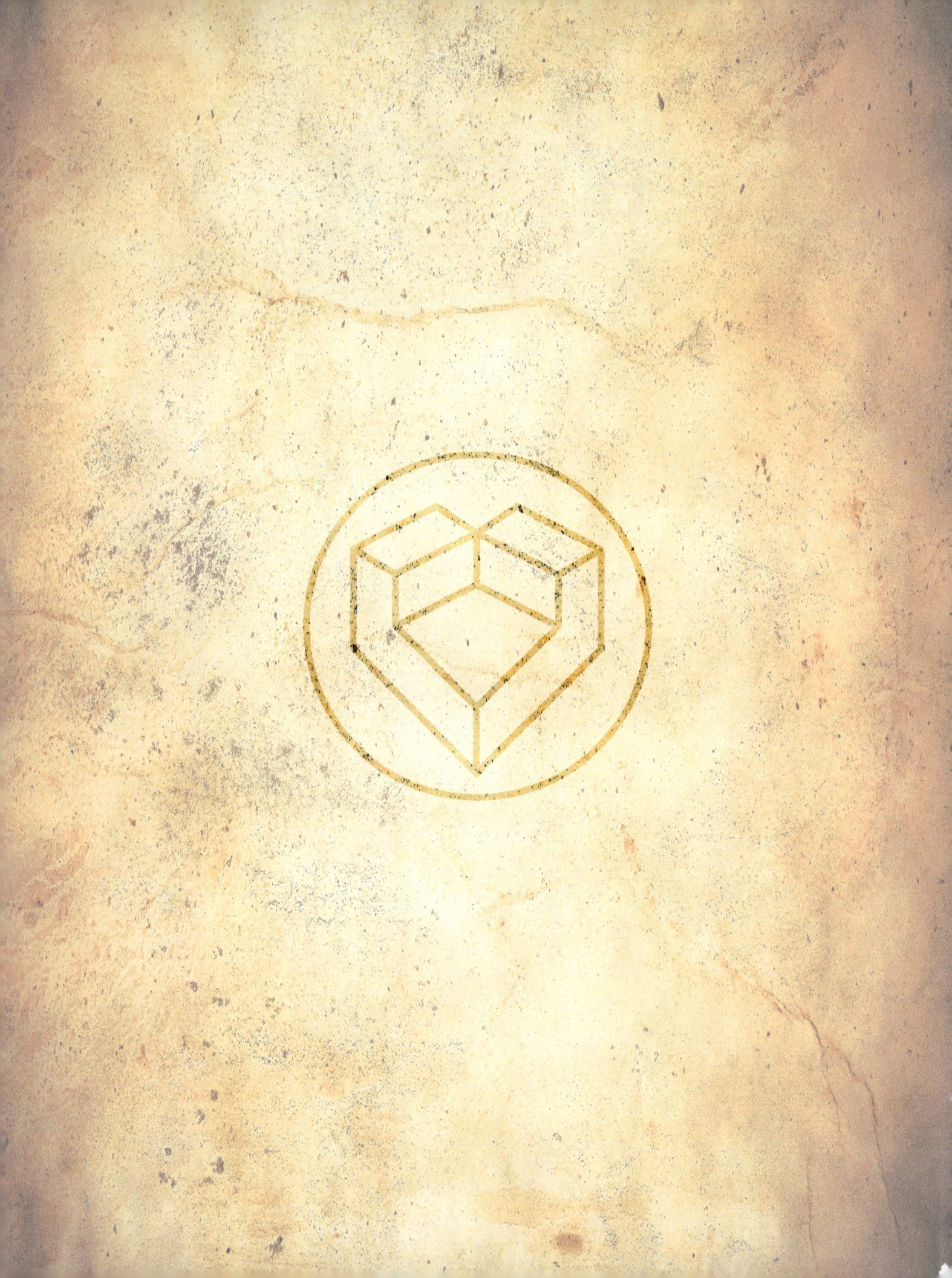

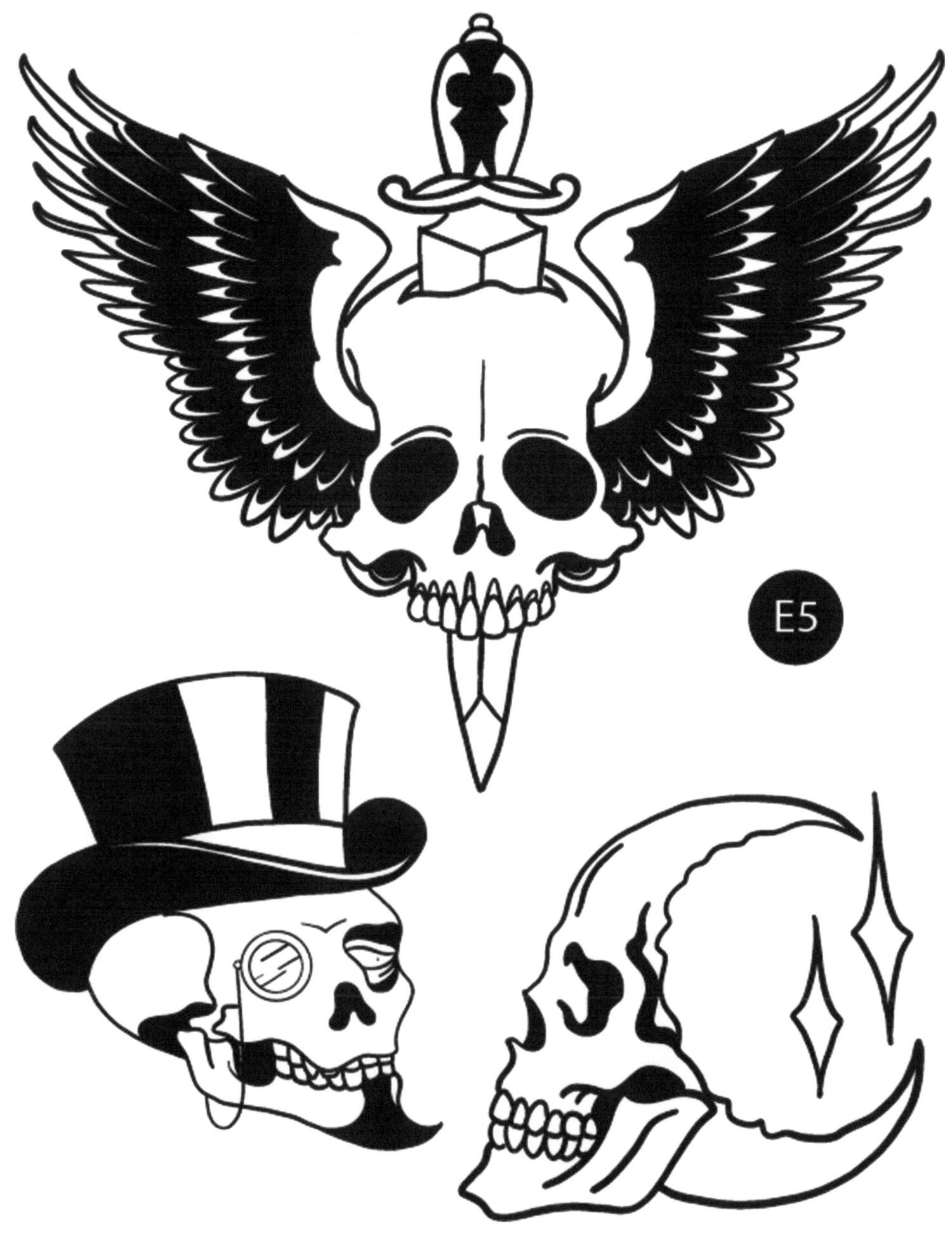

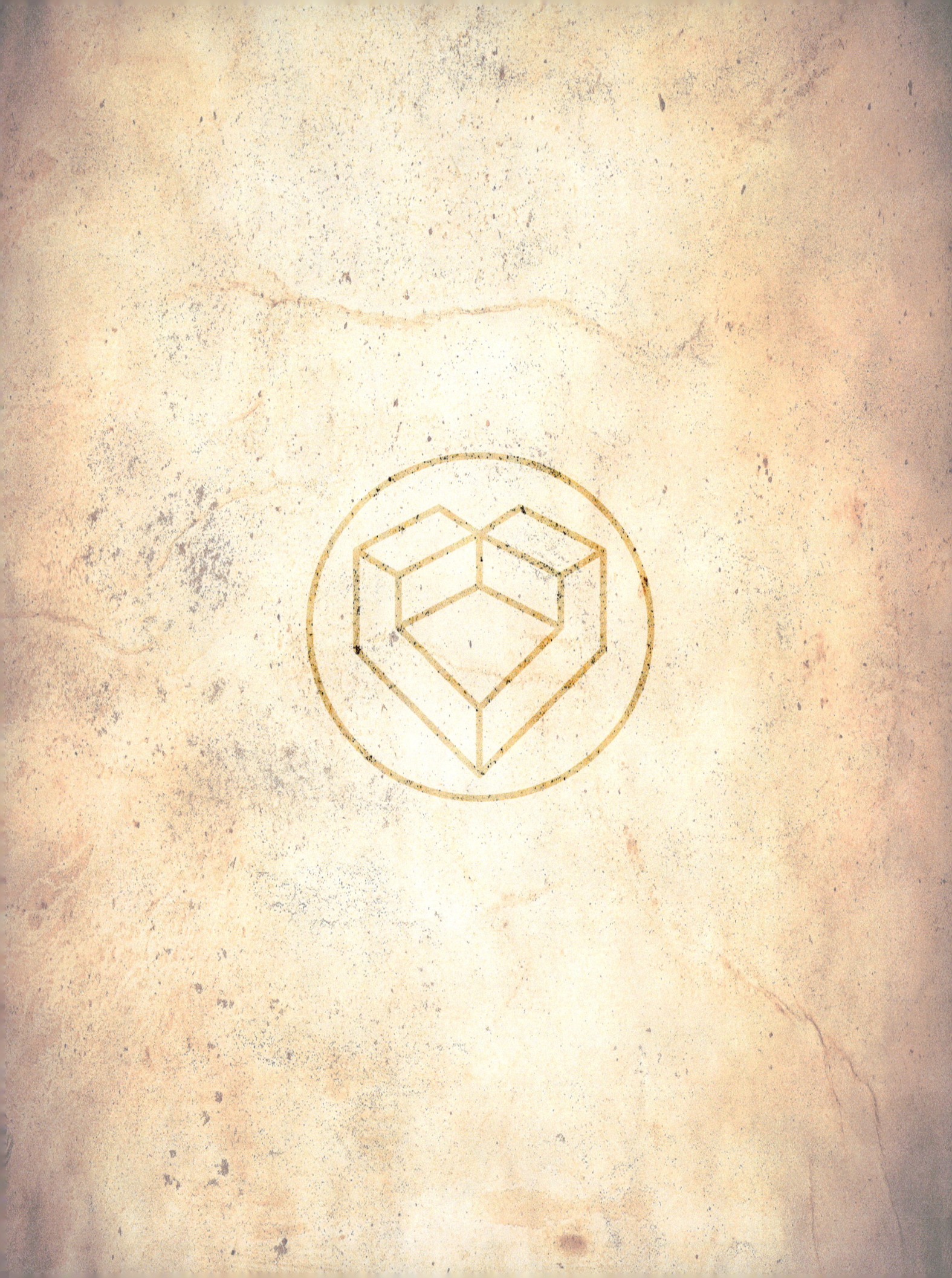

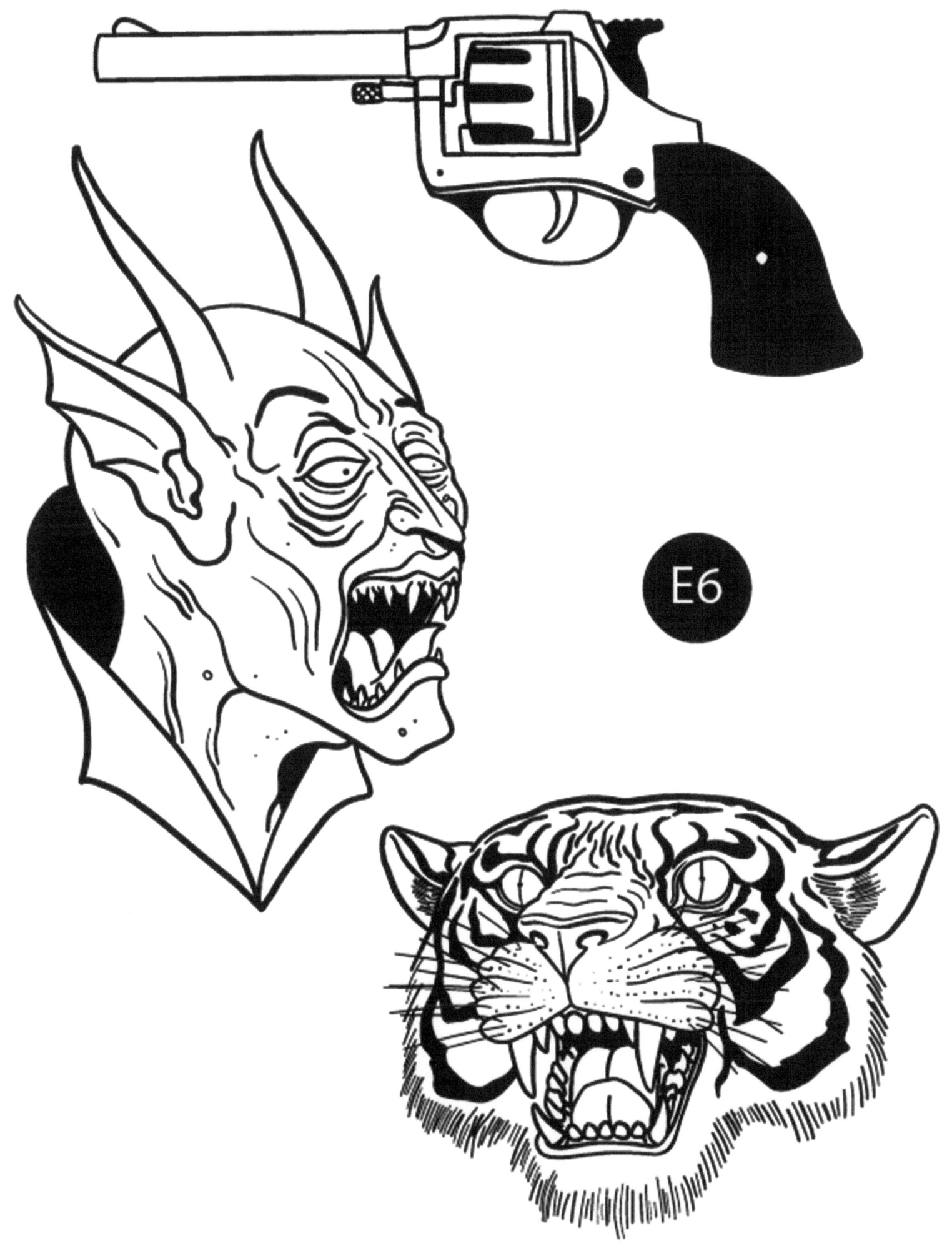

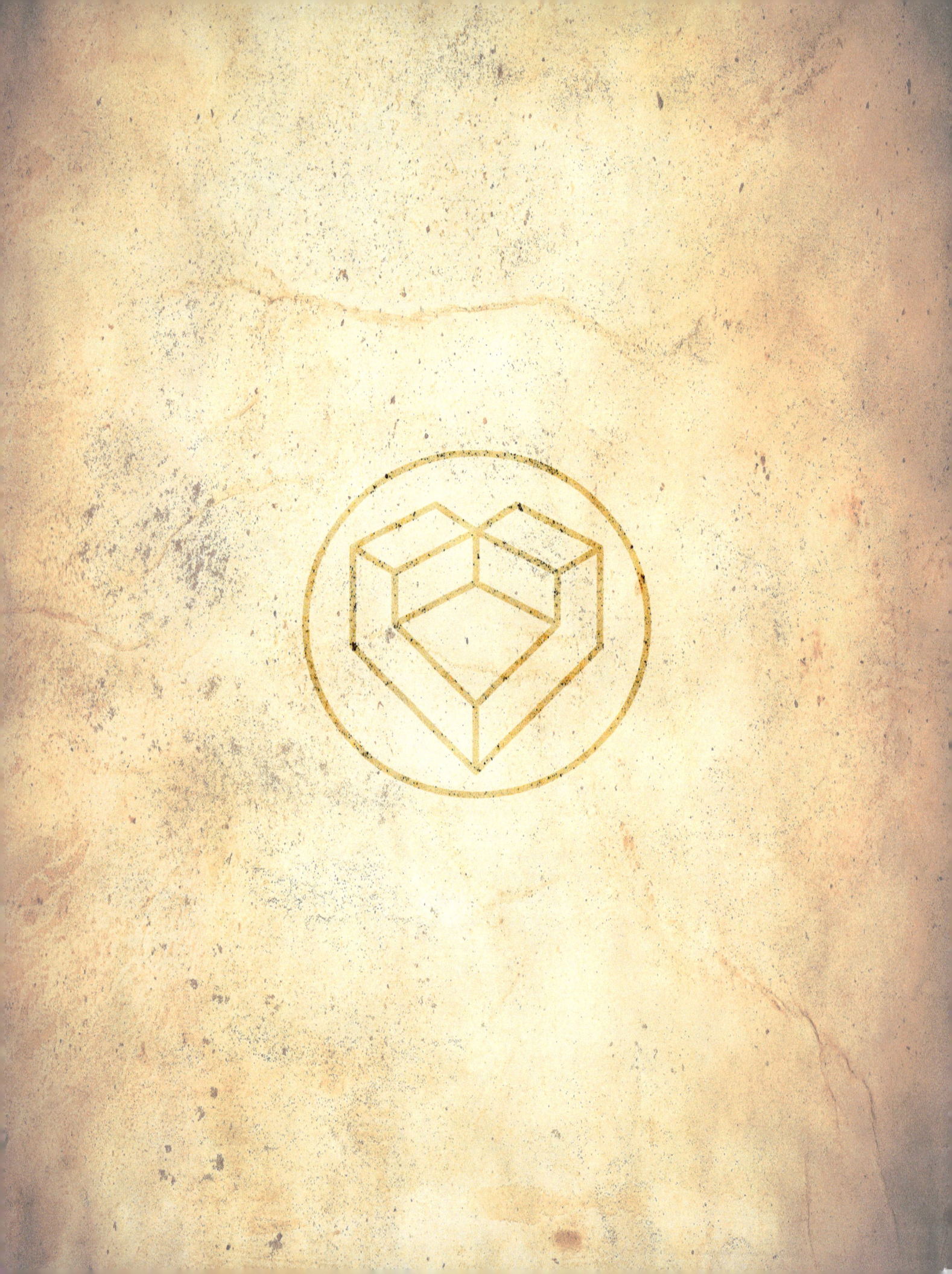

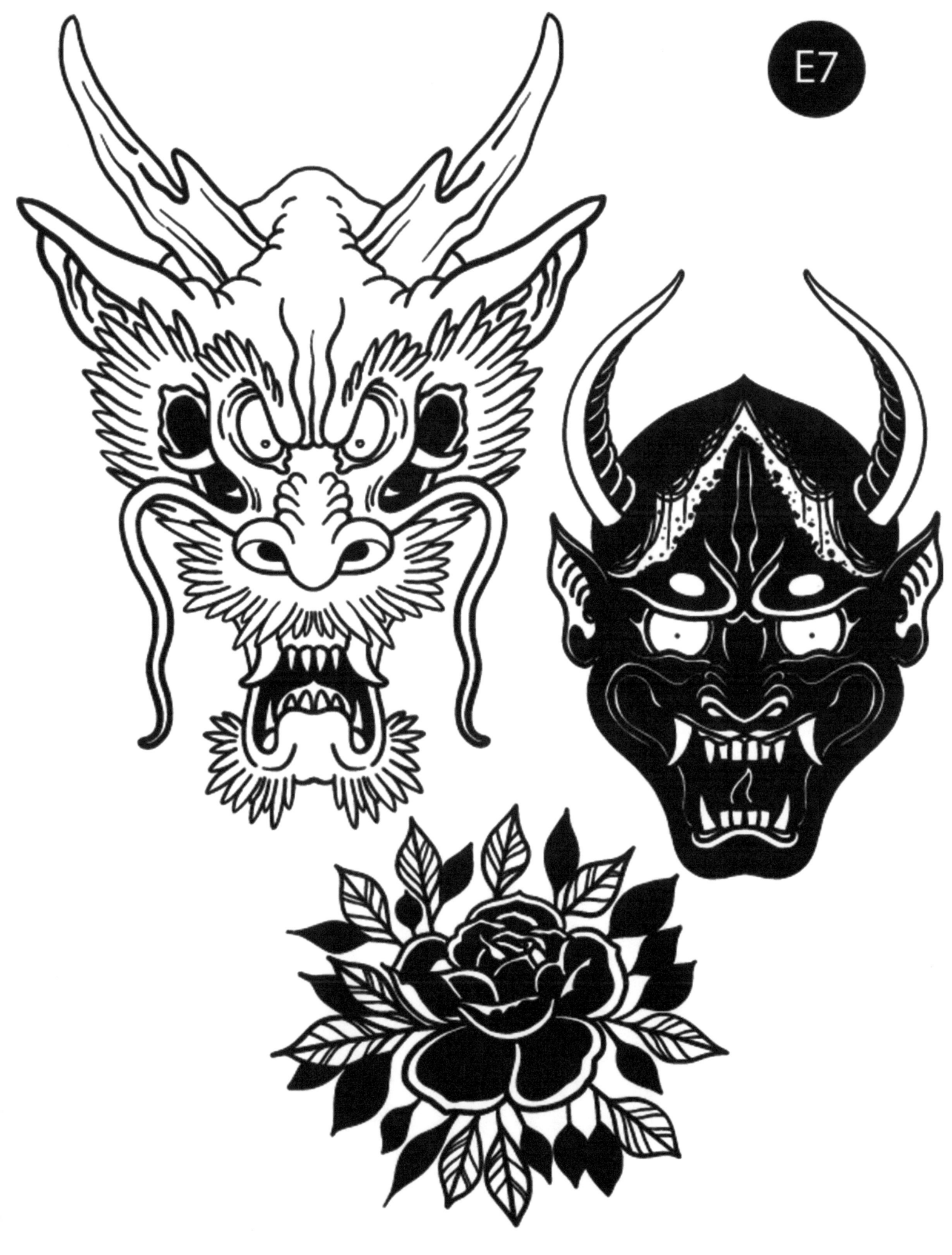

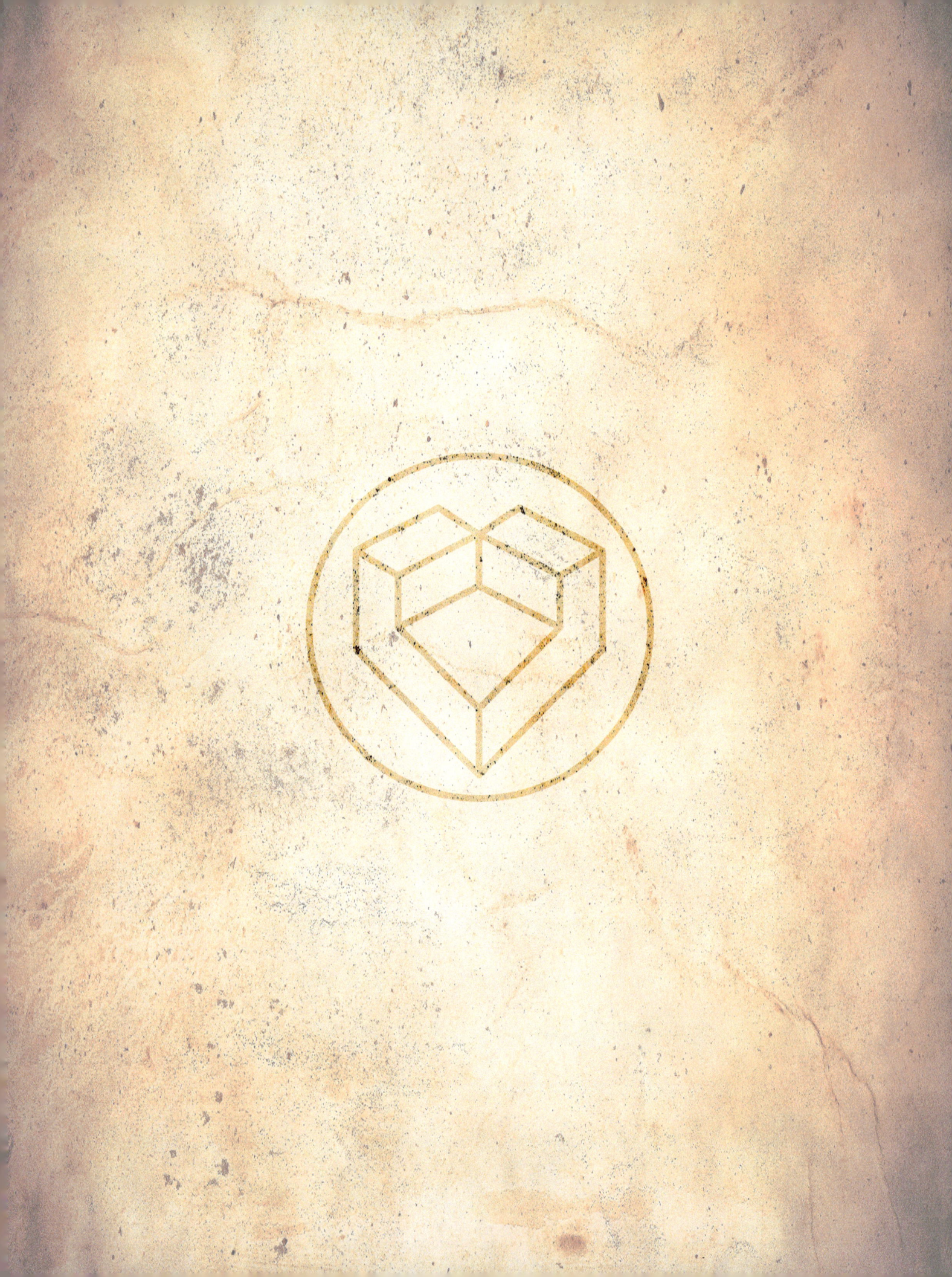

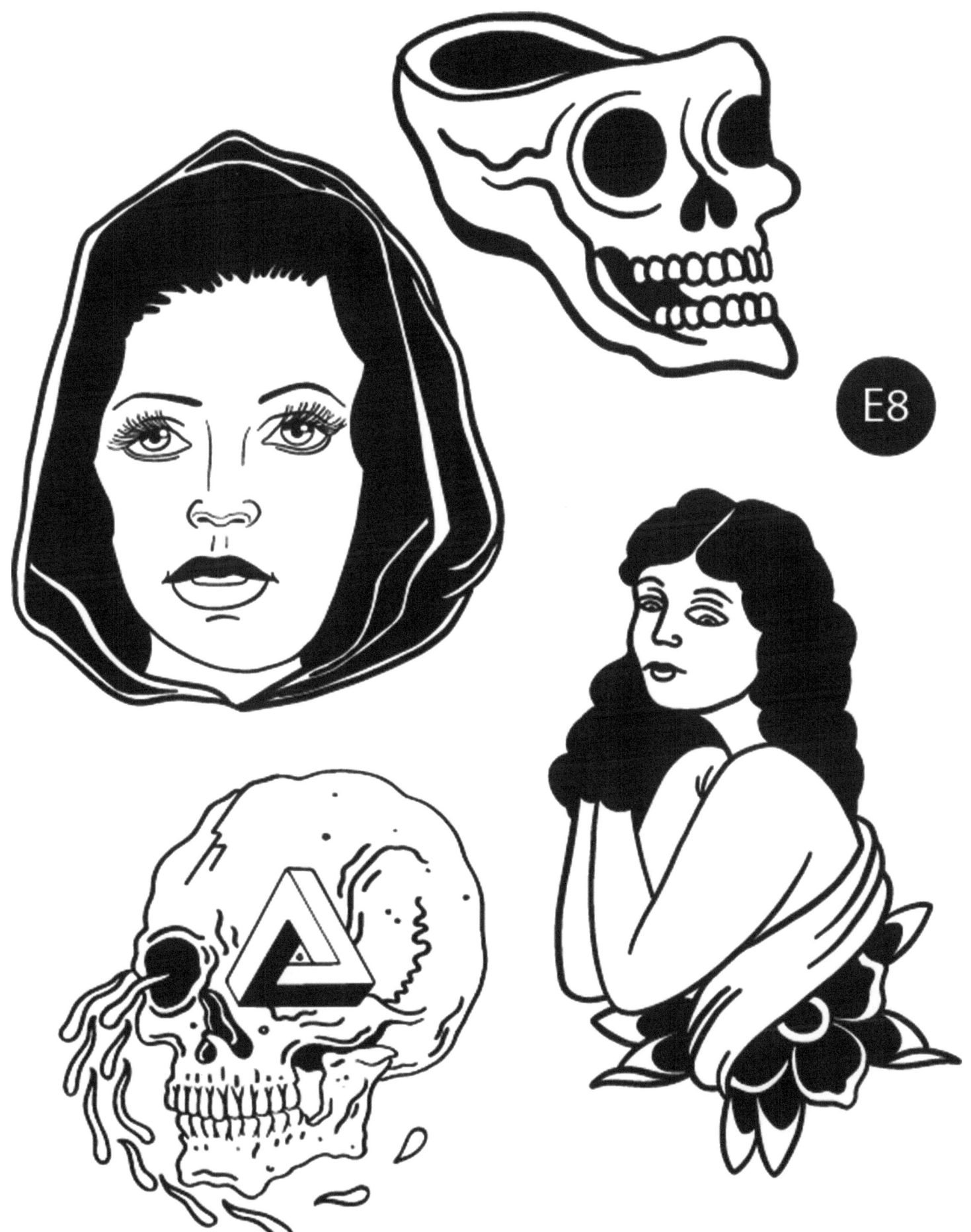

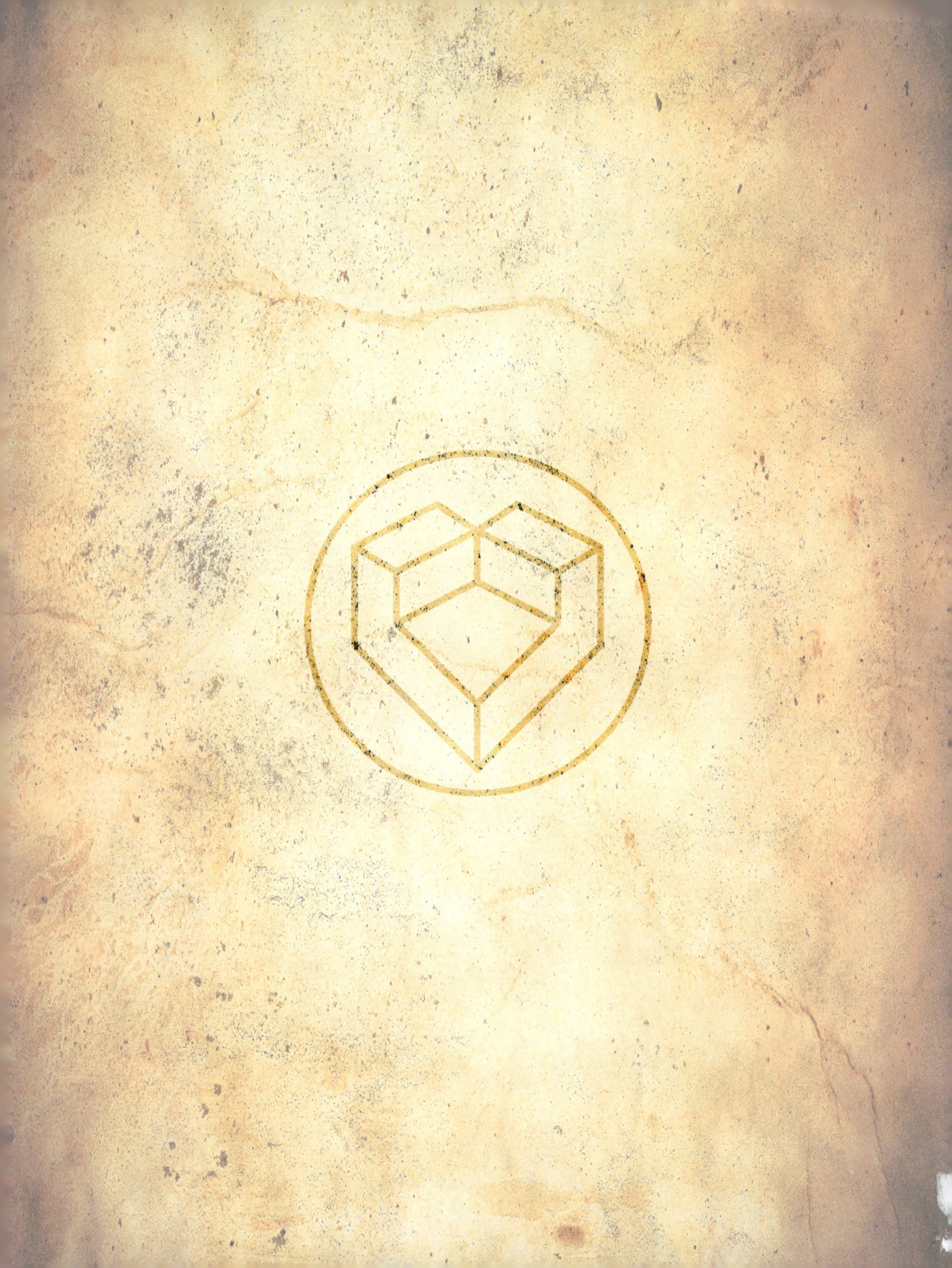

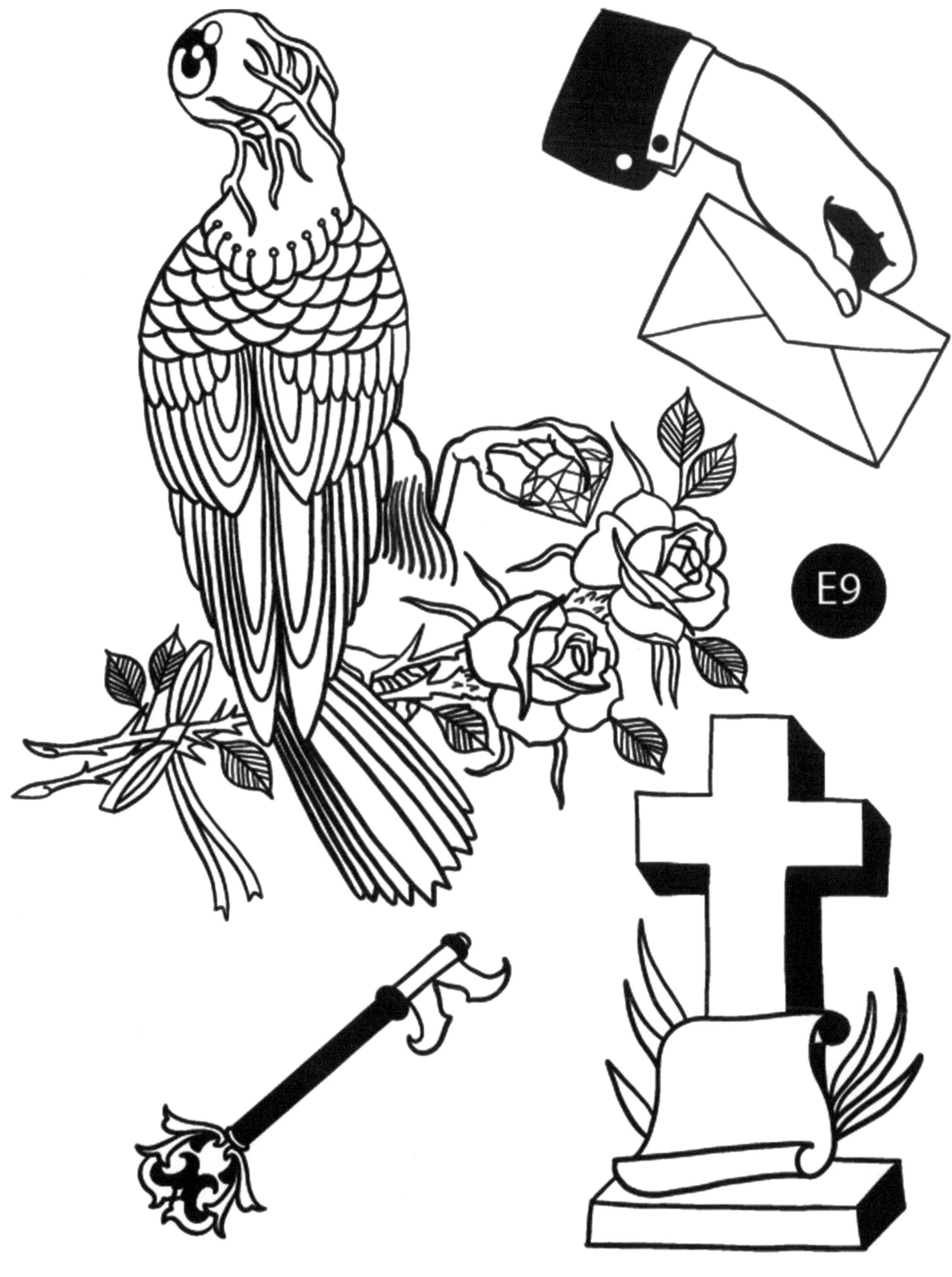

E9

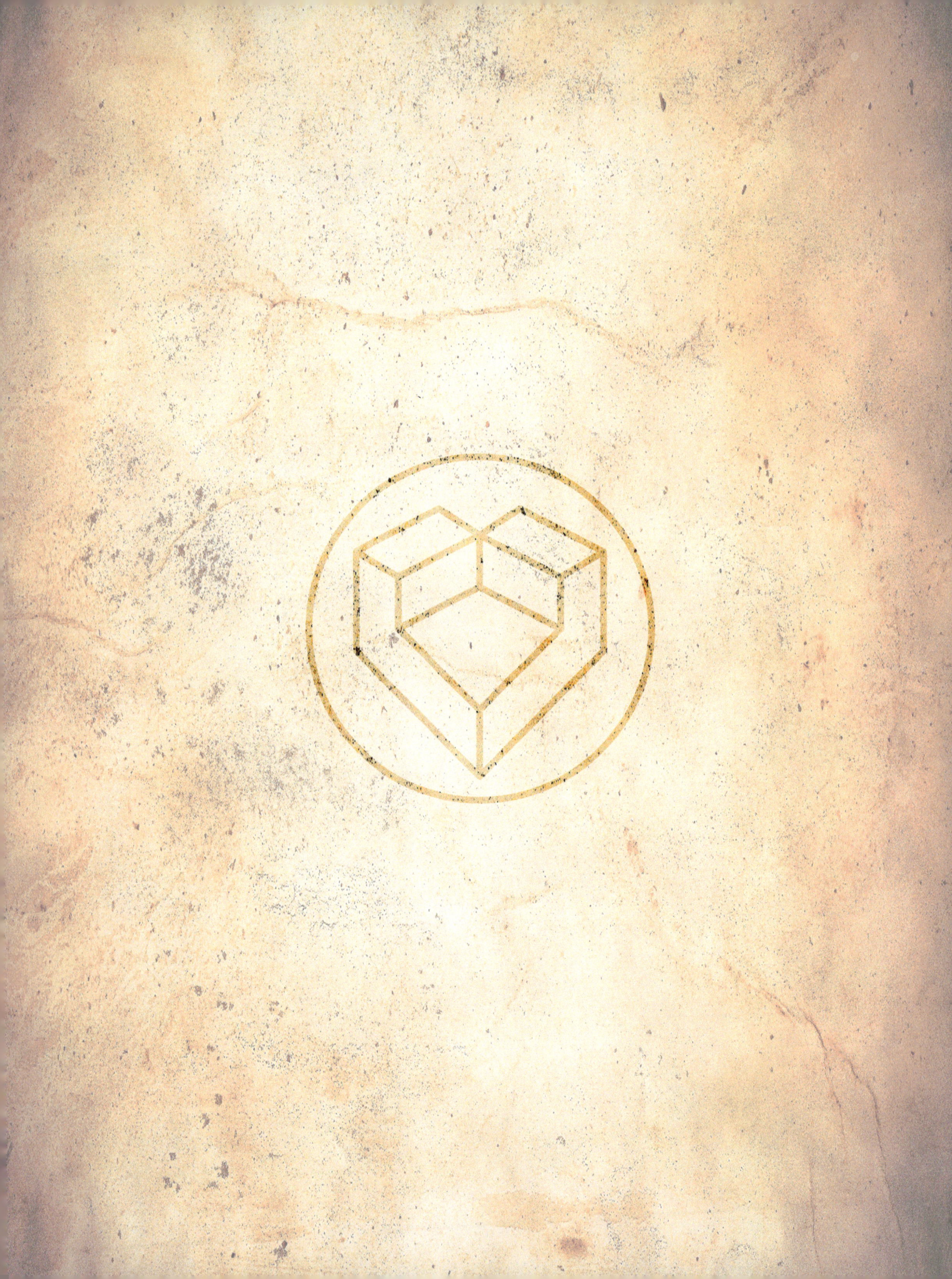